The Permissive Society

BOOKS BY THE SAME AUTHOR

Ernest Solvey, A Biography
Thomas Masaryk, A Biography
Edward Benes, A Biography
Napoleon, A Medical Biography
The "Mad" Philosopher: Auguste Comte
The Principles of Solvey's Positive Sociology
Vitality
The Revolt or The Quest
Bio-Dynamics of Man
Middle Age is What You Make It
The Civilized Diseases
Jealousy, A Psychiatric Approach
Science and The Purpose of Life
The White Nights
Unconquered Enemy
Cancer, New Approaches
The Story of Penicillin
The Miracle Drugs
The Achievement of Happiness
Carcinoid and Serotonin
The Permissive Society
On the Banks of the River Neva (in preparation)

THE PERMISSIVE SOCIETY

by

Boris Sokoloff, M.D., Ph.D.

ARLINGTON HOUSE   New Rochelle, N.Y.

303.4
SOK

1. Social change

Library of Congress Catalog Card Number 71-154417

ISBN 0-87000-132-9

MANUFACTURED IN THE UNITED STATES OF AMERICA

Foreword

• •

TEN years ago, this nation, great democracy that it is, was the most powerful country in the world. The principles of law, of self-reliance, the respect for individuality, and privacy, for man's stamina, and the acceptance of hard work as a basis of daily existence, were the motivating factors in the existence of the average American.

All this has changed almost overnight.

An extreme permissiveness, of an almost pathological nature, has engulfed a considerable part of the American population, not unlike a fast-growing cancer. Applauded, promoted, and fully approved by the liberal intellectuals, the permissive movement was declared by them as a social revolution, as the beginning of a new America. Permissiveness contaminated all sides of American life. Sociologists give poverty as the cause for an enormous increase in crime, with about 200,000 cases of forcible rape of women during the last eight years. Millions of young people, some of them still students in junior high and high schools, started to use narcotics, not limited to marijuana alone, and were condoned in their habits by authoritative intellectuals. Uncontrolled freedom of sex reached national proportions, with a growing and dangerous epidemic of venereal diseases. Riots erupted on university campuses all over the country, with many faculty members participating in and encouraging them. The pleasure-seeking instinct was declared a sign of a revolutionary attitude toward the establishment. Self-reliance, self-discipline, and desire for individual development were acclaimed as signs of a reactionary atavism, and were replaced by unrestricted permissiveness in the field of pleasure sensations.

Why has this country become so appallingly permissive? Our sociologists and political scientists, as well as many politicians, are inclined to interpret the permissiveness of this country as the result of social injustice and poverty of the masses or even of racial conflicts. The liberal intellectuals believe that once social reforms are realized, there will be no crime, no drug addicts, no campus riots, and no bombing of government and private buildings. Their reasoning is typically that of persons who received a liberal arts education and who utterly disregard the basic biological laws which direct human nature and humanity at large.

This book is an attempt to approach, from a biological point of view instead of from the unscientific concept of sociology, the incredible permissiveness confronting this country.

When I was planning to write this book, I discussed it with several faculty members at our Liberal Arts college. They were skeptical about my idea. These sociologists and political science professors strongly felt that I, a biologist and medical scientist, was intruding in their field, and that a biologist has no right to discuss the chaotic state of this country. In vain I tried to convince them that a biologist has more to say than a sociologist about deviations in human behavior, as long as human beings have inbred drives and reflexes, and that it is a great mistake for modern sociologists and political scientists to consider human beings as pawns in sociopolitical events. In spite of all their objections to a biologist's turning sociologist, and hesitant though I was, nevertheless I did decide to write this book, telling how a biologist sees the causes of the extreme permissiveness which affects our society and what physiological and biological factors are involved in it.

In this book I shall discuss the link between the Freudian ethic and American liberalism of today, both advocating permissiveness. And I shall emphasize the impact of Freud's rejection of religion on the permissive movement in this country.

Contents

PART ONE

•

FREUD:
The Apostle of Permissiveness

•

1

•

The Syndrome of Permissiveness

• •

WE are confronted in this country with what should be called the permissiveness syndrome. This psychological phenomenon, like a cancerous growth, is spreading rapidly over our population, affecting or infecting not only the younger generation but receiving an enthusiastic response from part of the older generation, mostly in influential intellectual circles. Its presence is evident in all aspects of our sociopolitical trends and man's existence. In education; in the judiciary system, with judges often manifesting an extreme permissiveness in their court decisions; in family life, often bringing tragedy and despair; in the extremes of sex; in politics; and even in religion, where many ministers and priests advocate permissiveness as a panacea for our society's ills and the pathway to a new and better life.

There is nothing new in the permissiveness syndrome. It was present in various forms and degrees during previous civilizations. As a rule it developed in nations which were in decline, in disintegration, or in serious troubles. As Arnold Toynbee stated in *A Study of History,*[1] in such nations there is a phenomenon which he calls "abandon."

"By *abandon* as an alternative to creativity in the lives of disintegrating civilizations, we mean something more precise than this primitive flux of feeling. We mean a state of mind in which antinomianism is accepted . . . as a substitute for creation." The absence of or decrease in creativity in the disintegrating nations leads to the diminution of purposefulness of man's existence, and subsequently of the nation itself. The prevalence of confused and contradictory words over creativity, the refusal to accept society as such without offering a substitute for it, gradually bring about the chaotic state in the affected society. And as the natural consequence of "abandon" in the affected nation, as an unavoidable part of it, there appears the permissiveness syndrome. Ancient Rome, the Babylonian Empire, and numerous other civilizations give a vivid picture of extreme permissiveness which actually contributed to their downfall. Promiscuity and excessive sexuality, unlawful behavior of citizens, growing crime and general use of narcotics, all this was a part of the permissiveness syndrome in past civilizations.

Yet, as was said before, there is considerable variation in the genesis and the type of the permissiveness syndrome. In this respect the so-called nihilistic movement in Russia about a century ago offers a peculiar undertone. It was strictly a university student movement. *Nihil* is Latin for "nothing," or in the Russian language *nichevo.* Russian nihilists were in appearance like the American hippies of today, with long hair, beards, and

[1]New York: Oxford University Press, 1947.

sloppy clothes. Not unlike American hippies, the majority of nihilists were sons and daughters of well-to-do parents. This movement based itself on the work of Darwin and Spencer which implied that possibly *homo sapiens,* man, is a descendant of the apes. If so, Russian youth concluded, then there is no God or Supreme Power. If there is no God, then all is permitted.[2] Thus an unlimited permissiveness was declared by the nihilists as the new religion. Yet, in the case of the nihilists, there was no emotional permissiveness. They were not interested in freedom of sex. They did not take part in orgies. They did not drink or take narcotics. They were avid readers and enthusiastic discussers. Yet they were against everything. Against any type of "Establishment," government, family, or church. Nevertheless, they respected their universities and made no attempts to destroy them. As critical as they were about everything, they did not try to improve the social–political situation in their country. In fact they were very passive, except for a small number of them who became activist revolutionaries.

Ivan Turgenev, the Russian writer of the nineteenth century, describes vividly in *Fathers and Sons*[3] the typical nihilist, Bazarov, who was very bright, quite conceited, and well-educated. Bazarov was challenged: "You deny everything; or speaking more precisely, you destroy everything . . . but one must construct too, you know."

"That's not our business . . . the ground wants clearing first," Bazarov answered. ". . . we decided not to undertake anything. . . . We confine ourselves to abuse. . . ."

"And that is called nihilism?"

"And that's called nihilism," Bazarov repeated, this time with peculiar rudeness.

---

[2]Fyodor Dostoevsky, *The Possessed,* London: Heinemann, 1956.
[3]Ivan Turgenev, *Fathers and Sons,* New York: The Heritage Press, 1941.

"But how destroy without even knowing why?"

"We shall destroy because we are a force," was Bazarov's answer.

When asked about the great artists and their creations, Bazarov was firm. "To my mind," he retorted, "Raphael's not worth a brass farthing; and they're no better than he."

Analyzing the constituents of the Russian nihilistic philosophy, one might find that there was an underground idealism, a despair of the conditions existing in their country at that time. As a reaction to this despair, a powerful negative feeling was born in them thus creating the phenomenon termed by Toynbee: *abandon*. Instead of creation there was a markedly pronounced negativism, associated with intellectual permissiveness. What distinguished Russian nihilism, with its limited permissiveness syndrome, was that there was no moral deterioration, no tendency for orgiastic behavior. There was a certain purity in this illogical movement.

The present-day permissiveness syndrome in this country is a complex phenomenon. We often hear that the youth movements are idealistic and revolutionary by nature. This is only partially correct, as is the statement about the existing gap between the two generations. The youth of today are criticized for their extravagances, their extremes in the interpretation of freedom, their promiscuity in sexual relations, for the campus riots and the absence of respect for law and order, for the use of narcotics. Yet the origin of the present permissiveness which affects a part of today's youth lies in the psychology and ethics of the older generation, specifically of the intellectual and quasi-intellectual circles. It is they who created the foundation for all that is now going on in this country, for they built the psychological premises for the behavior of our youth today. They are responsible for youth's confusion and revolt. They actually incited and are favoring the protests against the establishment, whatever this term means. No wonder the youth of today, at least some of them, are enchanted by the excitement which brings to them an unlimited permissiveness. They—the young —insist that there is a gap between them and their parents. But they do not realize that it is the older generation that made it possible for them to exploit the unlimited freedom which, in fact, is the product of American intellectualism.

Who are the young men and women who leave their homes and follow the hippies, or invade the administration buildings on a campus? The survey of hippies and rioting students indicates a remarkable fact. Seventy-eight percent of white hippies are sons and daughters of well-to-do parents, many of them belonging to the upper level of American society. Only 7.2 percent of them come from working class families. Many of the hippies willingly admitted that they had everything they wanted at their homes, but they were bored. They had been free to do whatever they wanted. They left their homes in search of new human values, they insisted, but they admitted also that there was an element of adventure in their decision to join the hippies. It is a revealing fact that a large part of the youth who become hippies or who participate in campus revolts belong to the upper and middle classes. No less impressive is the indication that the working class produces only a small percentage of hippies or campus rioters. It is an impressive fact, indeed, this close connection of student campus revolts and the hippie movement with the specific circles of our society: the professionals, the intellectuals, and the upper bourgeois class. Rebellious youth is an inseparable part of these groups of the older generation.

What is the permissiveness syndrome, biologically speaking? This is the most intriguing question one may ask. In order to understand the meaning of this term, we will draw an analogy with cancer. Everyone knows what cancer is—in a superficial way. All of us recognize that it is a dreadful disease which kills hundreds of thousands of humans every year. But the intrinsic process of cancerous growth is hardly known to the public at large. It is cytology, the science of cells, which offers us a fascinating picture of what is going on in our organism when this malady begins. If we take a piece of healthy tissue, not affected by cancer, and peer at it through a microscope, we see thousands of small cells arranged in perfect order—not unlike so many soldiers on parade. All of them, the healthy cells— vital, individual entities—each with a life of its own, remain in symmetrical ranks, as if trained by the most dogmatic of gener- als. There are many billions of cells which compose the human organism, and all of them, as long as they are healthy, not affected by cancer, exist in perfect obedience to the power which unites them, the power which we call morphogenetic power. The exact chemical nature of this power is unknown. We do know *in what manner* this power works. But no one is able to explain *why* this mysterious force is so powerful. Why should the cells obey its rule so completely and forgo the natural inbred desire of the cells to follow their stirrings for freedom and independence from the organism? They obey for the sake of the entity of their cellular kingdom. Thus, employing the modern- day slogan, we may say that in a healthy organism, its citizens, the cells, obey law and order to protect the vitality and life of the organism.

That is not the case with cancer. Let us take a small piece of tissue affected with what we call incipient cancer—a cancer which is just beginning to grow. If we look into the microscope, we see an extraordinary picture. Instead of the former orderli- ness and perfect coordination of cells, they now appear to be in a state of unmitigated chaos. Where once were orderly ranks of cells, now there is a profligate mob in helter-skelter confusion.

Some of the cells are crushed by their unbridled neighbors and are half-alive; others under unnatural stimulation are multiplying vigorously, unchecked and uncontrolled. The cancerous cells are trying to penetrate into the normal healthy tissue, surrounding some of the cells and destroying them. It is a revolt of cells which gained their complete freedom by rejecting the central governing power of the organism which held them in control. The rebellious cells, the cancerous ones, are possessed by a pronounced permissiveness syndrome. They do what their inbred drive for independence pushes them to do. We may say that cancerous cells flatly reject law and order.

Unless the incipient cancer, composed of rebellious and agitated cells, is exterminated either by surgery or x rays, the affected cells will travel in various directions of the human body, forming new nuclei of cancerous growth and gradually destroying and killing the organism.

Whatever the cause of cancerous growth might be—virus, chemical irritation, or hormones—the picture of the revolt of cells is the same.

One must admit that there is some analogy with a nation affected with an excessive permissiveness syndrome. The governing power of the nation is weakened. There is no longer law and order. A small but noisy group of rebellious citizens behave as if everything is permitted.

It is from the study of the revolt of cancer cells that one arrives at the conclusion that the permissiveness syndrome is an inbred property of a living organism and, unless it is controlled and restricted, the result might be the unavoidable destruction of the national entity.

The permissive syndrome is an atavistic characteristic of the human race. From time immemorial, when the first tribe was being formed and certain rules of conduct were imposed on the individual, man was obliged to follow those rules. Primitive man often protested. His inbred drive demanded that he have the right to do what he wanted. With growing civilization, the pressures and demands of society became more powerful and strict. Man's permissiveness syndrome was more repressed and subordinated to the rules of the society to which he belonged. Suppressed as it was, the permissiveness syndrome still remained a part of human personality. And, as was said before, the moment the structural power of a society was weakened, the syndrome was revitalized, an active factor in man's behavior and in a nation's destiny.

Thus we accept that a nucleus of the permissiveness syndrome is inbred in every human being. It is a desire for and drive toward unlimited freedom. It is a protest, often violent and vicious, against any limitation or restriction of freedom in any possible way.

Yet there are individual differences both in men and animals originating in inherited characteristics. Let us take, for example, two kinds of dogs—a police dog and a dachshund. Both are intelligent and lovable animals. Yet, while the police dog is willing to accept certain restrictions of freedom and, through training, controls his permissiveness syndrome, a dachshund objects to any restrictions on his freedoms or wants. A dachshund does what he wants to do. You may succeed in training him, yet he still refuses, occasionally, to be housebroken. He knows it is wrong. You may punish him, again and again, and the next day he will wet on your expensive carpet or on your bed or may do something even more drastic. Scientists who investigated the peculiar behavior of dachshunds arrived at the conclusion that their physical constitution, probably of a hormonal nature, is responsible for their unyielding permissiveness syndrome.

Let us now turn toward humans. A child two years old or younger is the bearer of a pronounced and absolute permissiveness syndrome. He does what he wants to do, as long as he is not restricted by his parents. He wets on the floor or bed, he destroys his toys or even some valuable *objet d'art* if he finds one. Thus this drive or instinct is essentially a primitive manifestation. It is a rejection or disregard of the society, small though it is, in which he lives. Parents who have several children soon find out that there is a considerable difference in the response of their individual children to the same restrictions on their freedom. Some children, like the police dog, soon accept the regulations imposed by their parents, while others stubbornly refuse for varying periods of time to control their freedom impulse.[4] Thus again we realize that the hereditary factor is of prime importance in the permissiveness syndrome control.

As the child grows, he develops his control of the permissiveness syndrome. It is a natural process, to which training and education are only contributing factors, and hereditary characteristics are still a dominating factor in the child's development, in his maturity, in the formation of his personality. He might be born in poverty, as millions of immigrants were, and still when reaching adulthood be in perfect control of his permissiveness syndrome. Yet if the child is growing up in a permissive society, as is the case of hundreds of thousands of children in this country, his self-control might be poorly developed or even altogether inhibited. And in the case of individuals with an excessive inbred permissiveness syndrome, we might be confronted with an abnormal psychology. Such an individual would easily be convinced that "all is permitted" to him, that he is a law unto himself. That is the basis of the formation of a criminal mind. His reeducation is often impossible. He is emotionally immature by nature; he does not possess the self-

---

[4]Benjamin Spock, the pediatrician, in *Baby and Child Care*, New York: Pocket Books, 1946, advised parents not to restrict the permissiveness complex of children. Spock, a Freudian, modified this advice in the later editions of this book, however.

control which would prevent his following the paths of extreme permissiveness. It is from this quite numerous group that criminals originate, because crime is the product of an uncontrollable permissiveness syndrome. The feeling that all is permitted to him is a drive stronger than himself, particularly if he lives in a permissive society. From this scientific premise one may doubt the rationality of the belief that poverty is the cause of crime. It is an insult to common sense to state that poverty is the cause of the numerous cases of forcible rape of women in this country.[5] It is not poverty which should be blamed for about 750,000 cases of car theft every year. And robberies which occur one every two minutes are mostly by professional criminals, as are the activities of the Mafia, of course. No one would suggest that its members are poverty-stricken. The cause of criminal behavior in a large number of cases can be traced to the influence of the inbred permissiveness syndrome, which is activated and will mushroom, if the society is unable or unwilling to repress the criminal's belief that all is permitted to him.[6]

We are now witnessing a fascinating phenomenon in this country. The "flower" of our society, the intellectuals and the wealthy, promote and defend an extreme permissiveness, without even realizing that they are contaminated by the Freudian ethic, the ethic which declares that all is permitted, that the permissiveness syndrome is the natural drive of a human being to be free from society, and that it should not be repressed or even controlled.

[5] *Crime in the United States, 1968*, issued by J. Edgar Hoover, August 1969.
[6] The cause of crime will be discussed in Chapter 7.

2
.

Freud in America

• •

THERE is a paradoxical phenomenon, the cause of which can only be defined with some reservation. Freud's teachings, or more properly his dogmalike theories, have little if any impact on life in European countries, or in fact in any other country of the world. However, Freud's influence in the United States is tremendous. Every aspect of American existence shows the imprint of Freudianism. All sides of our life are saturated with Freudian ideas and postulates.

Without any exaggeration one must admit that the impact of Freudianism on America is extraordinarily strong. Why has our country been so susceptible to the contaminations of Freudian ideas? And why did those countries where Freudianism originated, Austria and German, where much of the original work of Freud and his associates was published, remain immune to this teaching?

One is rather surprised by the fact that in Russia, Freud was rejected even before the communists seized power there. At present not a single scientific paper refers to his doctrine. Yet as an antireligious teaching, Freudianism should have been accepted enthusiastically in a country where religion was abolished. The same situation exists in the other countries behind the Iron Curtain. Neither Poland, nor Hungary, nor Czechoslovakia, nor Rumania gives any attention to Freudianism.

It seems that there are several factors which are involved in the extraordinary influence of Freud in this country, among them the natural reaction of intellectuals against American puritanism, the new concepts opened by Freud to writers and playwrights, and the considerable influx of Freudian fellows, psychoanalysts who emigrated from Europe to this country.

There are two periods or stages in the invasion of the United States by Freud. The first period was limited to a group of psychologists and literary people. It started with the visit of Freud, Jung, and Ferenczi to the United States in 1909. They were invited by Clark University, Worcester, Massachusetts, to participate in the celebration of the twenty-fifth anniversary of the founding of this university. Freud's visit to this country did not incite any popular interest and psychoanalysis remained unknown to the public at large for several years. In 1910 the American Journal of Psychology published articles by Freud, Jung, Jones, and others. Only a few psychologists accepted the Freudian doctrine. However, soon after his trip to America, Freud and his followers initiated an energetic promotion campaign. The most ardent supporter of Freud, A. A. Brill, was the first to bring the attention of the public to Freud, by publishing in 1913 Freudian articles on sex. This immediately stirred the attention of the intellectual circles. Numerous articles appeared in *Century, The Nation,* and *Dial.* Freud's theory and interpretation of dreams, always associated with sex, caught the imagination of the intellectuals. *The Nation* devoted several of its articles to the Freudian theory of dreams, remaining, however, quite skeptical about its soundness. The Freudian theory of dreams, *The Nation*'s editorial review stated, tended to "overemphasize the potency of erotic influence in all of experience, and in the field here considered the results of this preconception are conspicuous, leading to improbable and revolting explanations."[1]

It was Max Eastman, instrumental in glorifying Lenin and Soviet Russia in his books, who actually introduced Freud to the American public.[2] Not being trained either as a psychologist or a psychiatrist, Eastman presented Freudianism in the most attractive way, as a new body-healing discovery. He reported several cases of psychoanalysis which resulted, according to him, in the magic recovery of patients from their illnesses.

Eastman, a poet, described the unconscious mind as "a mysterious well of water, whose conscious surface is not large but which spreads out to great distances and great depths below." By giving such an unscientific description of the unconscious mind, Eastman contributed to the layman's acceptance of Freudian theories. Gradually, Freudian ideas reached Greenwich Village where they became a vogue, a subject of sharp discussions and appreciation, with Walter Lippmann and Mabel Dodge defending them and Warner Fite rejecting them. Fite denounced Freudianism as basically abnormal and obscene.[3]

For a few years, the magazine *The Masses,* edited by Max

[1] *The Nation*, 1913, pp. 594–5.
[2] Max Eastman, "Exploring the Soul and Healing the Body," *Everybody's Magazine,* 1914, *23*:741–50.
[3] Fite, Warner, "Psychoanalysis and Sex Psychology," *The Nation*, 1916, pp. 127–9.

Eastman and Floyd Dell, was the organ for militant Freudianism which soon became unavoidably associated with various
sociopolitical problems, such as divorce, and freedom of sexual
relations. Freudianism remained in vogue among Greenwich
Village intellectuals until Leninism and Soviet Russia replaced
it there. Yet the impact of the Freudian theory of sex on Greenwich Village intellectuals was considerable and lasting. It was
through the acceptance of the Freudian doctrine that Greenwich Village acquired the reputation of a sinful center of the
avant-garde of American intellectuals. Misinterpreted, mis-
guided, glorified, and criticized, Freud's doctrine spread from
Greenwich Village to larger intellectual circles and developed
into a topic of discussion as well as of personal involvement to
many Americans affected with neurosis, frustration, and ills,
imaginary or actual. Freudianism thus became a national problem which gradually affected the existence of millions of Americans.

Looking back to the embryonic period of Freudianism in
Greenwich Village, one is impressed by the fact that scientists,
biologists and psychophysiologists, or the medical profession,
were not impressed and interested in Freudian doctrine. The
scientists at large remained skeptical or indifferent to this movement. It was sociologists, social workers, and literary men who
were attracted to and excited by the new horizons opened to
them by Freud. Accepting the premises of Freudian theory
enthusiastically, they tried to find in it the confirmation of their
own sociopolitical beliefs and theories. No wonder Freudian
ideas became the subject of literary activity: The unconscious
drive of man and sexuality offered writers a rich and new
material for their fictional imagination. True enough, there was
nothing new in the concept of man's unconscious mind. Dostoevsky based all his creative literary work on the conflict between man's conscious and unconscious drivings. But never

before was the dichotomic nature of man so primitively simplified as by Freud. He presented the behavior of man in a
fascinating manner which, however, was hardly scientific per
se. As much as American literary men were intrigued by
Freudian ideas, they accepted them with some reservation and
hesitation. They were somewhat confused and bewildered.

The case of Theodore Dreiser is typical in this respect. On
several occasions I had the opportunity to discuss with him his
wholehearted approval of Freudian ideas. Dreiser believed that
Freud brought to this country what he termed "a psychological
revolution." The prejudices of our society, Dreiser would say,
will be reduced to ashes by this movement, which opens to the
creative literary mind a new pathway for a better understanding
of human nature. The freedom of sex was welcomed by him,
and he admitted that the sexuality, which served as a departing
point in his later novels, was a reflection of Freudian ideas. I
wondered how he could combine his acceptance of Freud with
his overwhelming adoration for Lenin's communism. I repeatedly told him that there was no common ground between Freud
and Lenin, except their atheistic credo. He was vague indeed in
explaining his double acceptance of these two so different teachings. His explanation was that they both were revolutionary
movements.

I also pointed out to him that there could not be a greater
difference in the personality of these two men: Freud, emotional
and vacillating, with a rich imagination, in fact with a too-rich
imagination, basically a neurotic, sensual, with the unconscious
mind dominating him; and Lenin, an analytic intellect, practical, calculating, self-controlled, indifferent to sex, with the unconscious completely suppressed by his conscious mind. And
their behavior was as far apart as were their personalities. To
Lenin, Freudianism would not only be foreign, but a revolting
speculation. Lenin, if he had known Freud, would have called

him a fool. But Dreiser was not convinced by my description
of his two idols.

Not unlike Dreiser, the majority of American novelists and
playwrights accepted part of Freudian doctrine, but Freud's
ethic, his negative philosophy, was not reflected in their creative
work.

Sexuality, of course, became a major element in the creative
activity of American literary men who believed that "sex" belonged to them. This interest in sex, somewhat mild and reserved in the beginning of American Freudianism, has reached
its peak in our times. In many thousands of books, the influence
of Freud can be detected easily and in some novels and plays,
Freudian ideas form the entire basis of the story. One finds
Freudian undertones in the work of Waldo Frank, Ben Hecht,
F. Scott Fitzgerald, and Sherwood Anderson; and in writers
such as Edward Albee, Tennessee Williams, Philip Roth, and
a multitude of others, the Freudian background is massively
pronounced. Yet when analyzing the most prominent literary
men affected by Freudian ideas, one observes considerable confusion in the manner of their acceptance of Freud. Sherwood
Anderson's novels offer rich material for understanding the
psychology of a writer confronted with this problem.

Not unlike Freud, Sherwood Anderson possessed a rich
imagination. Even in his memoirs, one has difficulty in separat-
ing reality from imaginary pictures. "When I had been working
well," he wrote once,[4] "there was a kind of insanity of consciousness. There may be little nerves in the body that, if we
could bear having them sensitive enough, would tell us everything about every person we meet." His description of his father
and mother is far from an accurate one of their actual personalities, with his mother complex strongly pronounced, as if his
unconscious mind had created their images.

[4] *Sherwood Anderson's Notebook,* New York, 1928, p. 183.

He belonged to the Greenwich Village of Chicago where, not unlike New York, a small group of intellectuals experimented with psychoanalysis. In the beginning he was quite ignorant about Freudian teaching. He was very frank about this period, writing about it much later: "Freud had been discovered at the time and all the young intellectuals were busy analyzing each other and everyone they met. Floyd Dell was hot on it. They had gathered in the evening in somebody's room. Well, I hadn't read Freud (in fact I never did read him) and was rather ashamed of my ignorance. . . . They psyched me. They psyched men passing in the street. It was a time when it was well for a man to be somewhat guarded in the remarks he made, what he did with his hands."[5]

Much of Freudian theory was based on Freud's personal experience. In this approach, of course, any scientific element was often disregarded. In fact Freud advised his patients and friends that "amateurish analysis" should be conducted by persons untrained in psychoanalysis. It is apparent that the type of "psyching" that Anderson described was quite popular in the intellectual circles of his time. The scientific value of such "psyching" was not only confusing but misleading. But, as Freud remarked, it served to popularize psychoanalysis.

Yet reading the memoirs of Sherwood Anderson, one feels that the term "American Freudian," applied to him by the critics, is hardly justified.

An almost similar case is that of Eugene O'Neill, preoccupied with sex and neurosis in his plays. He complained about the critics who emphasized the influence of Freud in his works. They see, he argued, Freudianism in everything.

"They read too damn much Freud," O'Neill wrote,[6] "into stuff that could very well have been written exactly as it is

[5]*Sherwood Anderson's Memoirs,* New York, 1942, p. 243.
[6]Barrett Clark, *Eugene O'Neill: The Man and His Plays,* New York: Dover Publishers, 1947, pp. 136–7.

before psychoanalysis was even heard of. Imagine the Freudian bias that would be read into Stendhal, Balzac, Strindberg, Dostoevsky, etc., if they were writing today." He admitted, like Sherwood Anderson, that he was not a student of Freud and had read only a few of his books. "I'm no deep student of psychoanalysis. As far as I can remember of all the books written by Freud, Jung and others, I have read only four, and Jung is the only one of the lot who interests me. Some of his suggestions I find extraordinarily illuminating by the light of my own experience with hidden human motives." And he stressed that "there is no conscious use of psychological material in any of my plays. All of them could easily have been written by a dramatist who had never heard of the Freudian theory and was simply guided by an intuitive psychological insight into human beings and their life impulses that is as old as Greek drama. . . . It was my dramatic instinct and my own personal experience with human life that alone guided me."

In spite of O'Neill's protests against the influence of Freudianism, an analysis of his plays fully shows that the impact of this theory on his creative activity was very strong. Yet one might concede that this influence was somewhat superficial, or rather that only certain points in Freudianism left an imprint on his work, and that Freudian ethics, the most essential part of Freud's concept of human life, remained untouched. O'Neill largely used neurotic manifestations as associated with sex.

The influence of Freud on O'Neill's writing is particularly evident in his play *Desire Under the Elms*. There is some similarity between the play's basic idea and Freud's *Totem and Taboo*. In both cases, females are dominated by powerful and strong fathers who send away their young sons, who at the end kill their fathers. In 1927, when O'Neill was having marital difficulties, he underwent psychoanalysis with Dr. Gilbert V. Hamilton, a Freudian. O'Neill was drinking heavily and was unable to stop. Shortly thereafter, he wrote *Strange Interlude.* Fritz Vittels[7] found a great impact of Freud on O'Neill's *Mourning Becomes Electra* and believed that this play showed a profound knowledge of Freud's incest complex. All in all, reviewing numerous plays of O'Neill, one arrives at the conclusion that, in spite of the author's protests, the impact of Freud and Jung on his creative activity was very strongly pronounced.

The Freudian theory of dreams was exploited by several playwrights, among them John Howard Lawson in his play *Roger Bloomer.* There he actually staged all the dreams, distorted as they were, in all their complexity. As attractive and intriguing as Freudianism appeared to American playwrights, some became dissatisfied with their attempts to use this theory in their plays. Elmer Rice, starting with *The Adding Machine* and *Dream Girl,* embodied Freudian ideas but ended with a much more realistic play, *Grand Tour.*

It is not my intention to describe in detail the impact of Freudianism on the American novel and drama. I have mentioned only a few early examples to demonstrate the superficial nature of the adaptation of Freudian concepts by American literary men. David Siever[8] and Frederick J. Hoffman[9] gave excellent reviews of almost all leading writers and dramatists. From their reviews it appears that the Freudian influence was considerable although somewhat questionable in many instances. There seems to be little if any doubt that American authors and dramatists prepared the ground for the invasion of America by Freud. But the large masses of the population were still not affected by Freudian ideas. There was a certain interest

[7]Fritz Vittels, *Psychoanalysis and Literature: Psychoanalysis Today,* New York: Covici-Friede, 1933, pp. 347–8.

[8]David E. Siever, *Freud on Broadway,* New York: Hermitage House, 1955.

[9]Frederick J. Hoffman, *Freudianism and the Literary Mind.* Baton Rouge: Louisiana University Press, 1945.

in them, some curiosity, and a good deal of discussion, but the Freudian ethic, his negativism, his defense and promotion of extreme permissiveness had not reached the consciousness of Americans.

The deep-seated impact of Freud on the American way of life and mentality became evident in the thirties when a large part of the population accepted psychoanalysis as a vogue or fad. This occurred after numerous psychoanalysts immigrated to the United States from Europe. The second and most effective period of what is called the Freudian revolution was in swing.

The number of persons who have undergone psychoanalysis in this country during the last three decades and longer is enormous. The available figures, while not exact, indicate that the unconscious minds of more than two million Americans have been subjected to lengthy analysis. At a national meeting of the American Psychoanalytic Association in Los Angeles in 1967, the pathways of the growing influence of Freudian ideas on American life were made clear. It was stressed that most of the patients of psychoanalysts are teachers, social workers, economists, sociologists, artists, writers, and other highly educated professional persons. These patients are people who can have and actually do have considerable influence on the lives of others, on their children, on their wives, or husbands, and, as educators, teachers, or writers, on the masses of Americans, and on our sociopolitical trends. A survey conducted by the Association showed that a large proportion of psychoanalytic patients are college educated and many have graduate degrees. Blue-collar workers, laborers, and farmers have escaped Freudian therapy—perhaps because psychoanalysis is the most expensive therapy ever known in this country.

About 60 to 65 percent of all patients are women. In her

famous play *The Women,* Clare Boothe Luce gave a vivid picture of the times—the thirties—when psychoanalysis became a fashionable fad for those wealthy women, satisfying their urge for attention and excitement and sex. They found great satisfaction in demonstrating their spiritual nudity. They were overjoyed with the seances with often youngish, soft-spoken psychoanalysts. This fad initiated by spoiled wealthy women gradually reached a larger group of females, the social workers, the teachers, the housewives, dissatisfied in their marriages. It became a national fad, limited, however, to the middle and upper classes.

The trend toward associating Freudianism with sociopolitical problems—which already was in evidence even in the days of the Freudian Greenwich Village—progressed on a wide scale. Teachers and educators started to apply Freudian postulates to education. Social workers, psychoanalyzed or not, started to promote Freudianism in their work and in welfare problems. Sociologists, who felt powerless at the time when heredity was declared a major factor in man's evolution, discovered in Freudianism a support for the significance of environmental factors. This approach became with them a departing point for endless environmental studies on rats, on dogs, and most of all on human beings. Hundreds of papers appeared in the American journals on the overpowering role of conditions of environment in the solution of society's ills. Even members of the judiciary system have not escaped the Freudian impact. In one of the chapters of this book, I analyze criminal court decisions as well as the Supreme Court rulings in the light of Freudian postulates.

One of the most impressive effects of Freudianism was on American liberalism. As long as the intellectual circles of our country responded favorably and enthusiastically to this teaching, many basic ideas of American liberalism, as formulated and defended by Woodrow Wilson, William English Walling, and other men and women of the past, were now rejected and even ridiculed by a new generation of liberals. Actually the Freudian revolution became synonymous with the American liberalism of today, although possibly many liberals would protest violently against such an assumption. It was also unavoidable that many politicians, Democratic and Republican, began to use Freudian language and ideas without even recognizing their close association with Freud.

Massive psychoanalysis in this country, unknown in any other nation, brought about the extraordinary success of Freud on a national scale. His success, or we may call it a victory, was and is much more formidable than that of Leninistic Marxism. In spite of persistent and clever propaganda by the communists, their influence never reached the masses of the population or even the American intellectuals to the same extent as Freudianism. The answer to this puzzle lies in the fact that psychoanalysis is not an impartial medical or psychological therapy. The method of psychoanalysis requires that the patient be persuaded, or trained, to accept fully and unreservedly the Freudian philosophy. Using the popular term of brainwashing, we may say that it is the base of psychoanalytic therapy. Again and again in his numerous seances, the psychoanalyst impresses on his patient the basic ideas of Freud. At the end of one or two years of psychoanalysis, the patient becomes convinced of the greatness of the Freudian doctrine. And in most cases of psychoanalysis, he declares himself a faithful Freudian follower. And incidentally, that was exactly the "promotion" plan of Freud himself. Here, he would say to his adepts and students, is the only way to introduce his postulates to large masses of the population: through close personal contact and repetitous implantation of the ideas in individuals. Freud used the "conditioned reflex" method of Professor Pavlov in his promotion campaign.[10]

Men or women, insecure and involved in personal conflict, often of a matrimonial nature, are affected by what we call a "swollen ego." They are so engrossed in their own inner conflicts that they cannot think of anything but themselves. Practicing physicians, and even some psychiatrists, believe that the best therapy in such cases is to advise the patients to direct their attention to some creative channels, and thus to reduce the "swollen ego" to nothingness. Psychoanalysis defends an opposite approach. It demands that patients talk and think about themselves. The psychoanalyst leads patients to the time of their youth, their mischiefs, their sins, their relations with their parents and specifically the recounting of their sexual lives. Thus from a psychological viewpoint, the analyst incites the "swollen ego" to grow even more, with the result that patients concentrate more and more on themselves. The patients develop an enormous "swollen ego." They are now self-centered more than ever before, conceited, and selfish. Psychoanalysts' efforts are directed to prove to patients that they are right, that there is no reason to blame themselves for anything they have done, and, in the case of most women, that the fault is with the husband. Often psychoanalysts insist that the husband should be included in the seance.

The net result is evident. Under pressure of the analyst, the husband feels guilty, the woman is right. No wonder psychoanalysis—since it has been used on a wide scale in this country, with millions of women psychoanalyzed—has unavoidably

---

[10]Ernest Jones, official biographer of Freud, mentioned that some of Freud's friends suspected that he himself did not believe in some of his own sensational postulates. He used them to stir the attention of the public to his work. There is no question that Freud was an excellent promoter of his own teachings.

created the guilt complex. The guilt complex, so foreign to Americans, is strongly pronounced in intellectuals and in the upper level of our society. The guilt complex is an essential part of the Freudian revolution and of the American liberalism of today, associated with the feminizing transformation of American males which is growing more and more pronounced as time goes by.

Paradoxically, however, we are confronted with an extraordinary phenomenon. While the influence of Freudian philosophy and ethics is growing fast, becoming an essential ingredient of our social structure, Freud's child—psychoanalysis—as a psychotherapy of emotional disturbances and neurosis, seems to be dying, if not already dead.

Dr. Bruno Bettelheim, one of the prominent figures in American psychoanalysis, recently called the major theoretical structures of Sigmund Freud, "time-bound, very shaky, very dubious.

"Freud's big theoretical abstractions, thrown out in a playful, ironical way, are now taken as dogma," he said. Comments of this nature—particularly the charge of inflexible unscientific dogmatism, once confined to bitter critics—are now commonly heard at the highest levels of psychoanalysis.

Many analysts agree that popular interest in psychoanalysis has declined in the last ten years. In addition, there are several other signs that suggest many troubles in this field of psychotherapy.

As an example, psychoanalysis is the least used of the approximately 30 recognized forms of psychiatric therapy in the United States, according to a survey by the National Institute of Mental Health. It reaches only two percent of psychiatric patients and that percentage is diminishing.

As the mental health field expands rapidly, psychoanalysis is losing ground to quicker, cheaper therapies that can reach low-income Americans who want psychological help. The high cost of psychoanalysis is also a detrimental factor. At $15 to $50 a session, three to six times a week for several years, psychoanalysis can often cost an individual $15,000 to $20,000. Also many critics charge that the lack of substantial research and theoretical development since Freud's death in 1939 has resulted in stagnation and lost impetus. "Almost everything we know about psychoanalysis today," said Dr. F. C. Redlich, Dean of the School of Medicine at Yale University and a Professor of Psychiatry, "was Freud's single-handed and single-minded word."

A powerful blow against psychoanalysis was struck by the impressive progress in the field of psychopharmacology. Abundant and scientifically sound material has been collected which firmly indicates that man's behavior, his mental aberrations, and even his more serious mental diseases can be and are affected, negatively or positively, by chemical substances, some of them of a metabolic nature. Not only is the role of endocrine disturbances in nervous ailments now well-determined, but numerous papers have appeared on neuro-hormones, including serotonin, a metabolitic substance.[11]

The most important discovery along these lines was reported recently by Stanford University psychiatrists.[12]

Dr. Keith Brodie, assistant professor of psychiatry, said six patients—all with a form of suicidal depression—have been treated successfully in the first pilot study.

The first patient was a woman who attempted suicide eight

[11]Boris Sokoloff, *Carcinoid and Serotonin.* Springer Publications, 1969.
[12]Harry Nelson, *Los Angeles Times,* December 28, 1970.

times in four months. All but one of the other five had also tried
to kill themselves. All have improved dramatically since treatment.

The patients he has been working with fail to produce enough
of an important brain chemical called serotonin. These patients
suffer from an affliction called agitated depression. Unlike some
depressed people who sit in a corner and never speak, the
serotonin-deficient patients continually pace the floor in an agitated manner and repeat over and over how worthless they are
and that there is nothing for them to live for.

The Stanford team measured the level of a chemical called
5-HIAA, in the spinal fluid of these patients. A breakdown
product of serotonin, 5-HIAA would be expected to be low if,
as the team speculated, the depression was caused by a lack of
serotonin.

They found the level of the chemical was indeed low—about
one half that found in normal persons.

The doctor then gave the patients a chemical called 5-
hydroxy-tryptophane, which the body can use to make serotonin. Within about five days, Brodie said, the patients' behavior
changed—they stopped the pacing and agitation, became much
less depressed and suicidal and began to eat and sleep normally.

At the same time their behavior changed, new readings of the
5-HIAA level revealed that they were now normal, indicating
that the behavior change resulted from restoring the serotonin
level.

This work fully corresponds to what we have known previously about serotonin. Once more this discovery indicates that
science is entering a new era in terms of looking at behavior
changes and relating them to the "internal environment" instead of accentuating the role of the external environment. It
shows that many mental diseases might be cured by biochemi-

cal factors instead of psychoanalysis or other forms of psycho-therapy.

The disciples of Freud have given to the world the image of Freud as a genius and a great scientist. In the next chapter, we describe Freud as he actually was, basing our sketch on the biography of Freud by his official biographer, Ernest Jones,[13] and on Freud's autobiography.

[13]Ernest Jones, *The Life and Work of Sigmund Freud,* New York: Basic Books, 1961.

3

.

Freud as a Scientist

• •

IT was March 1884. A 28-year-old resident of the Department of Nervous Diseases, Vienna General Hospital, came across an article published in a German journal by an Army doctor, Theodor Aschenbrandt. This paper attracted the attention of the young physician. Dr. Aschenbrandt reported that he had tried the alkaloid named cocaine, newly isolated by the Merck Company of Darmstadt, on some Bavarian soldiers during the autumn maneuvers and had found that a small dose of this drug increased their energy. The hospital resident, Sigmund Freud, saw in the properties of this alkaloid a chance to make his name known. As his biographer remarked: "During the three hospital years, Freud was constantly occupied with the endeavor to make a name for himself by discovering something important in either clinical or pathological medicine." And he explained that "his [Freud's] motive was not, as might be supposed, simply professional ambition, but far more the hope of success that would yield enough prospect of private practice. . . ."[1]

The first thing that Freud did was to purchase cocaine from Merck. He began to take it himself, by mouth, 50 milligrams a day, and he declared that the drug increased his energy and diminished his stomach troubles. On the basis of his personal experience he was so enthusiastic that he advised everyone to take cocaine: his fiancée, Martha Bernays, his sister, and his colleagues. He used cocaine to treat his friend, Ernst von Fleischl-Marxow, whose right thumb had been amputated due to an infection, and who continued to suffer terrible pain from the growing neuroma. Since Fleischl-Marxow was taking morphine, Freud decided to replace it with cocaine. "In short," Freud's biographer wrote, "looked at from the vantage point of our present knowledge, he was rapidly becoming a public menace."

On the basis of his own meager personal experience and that of one patient treated by him, Freud decided to write a paper promoting cocaine, the "magical drug," as he called it. He did write a paper in popular style, full of enthusiastic expressions —for example, that animals injected with cocaine displayed "the most gorgeous excitements." The paper, outlining the story of cocaine, extracted from the coca plant, was published in the July 1884 issue of *Centralblatt für die gesammte Therapie.* The paper was received by the German and Austrian medical profession with considerable interest. But Freud's fame from this discovery was somewhat obscured by the fact that two of his colleagues, to whose attention he had brought the re-

[1]Ernest Jones, *The Life and Work of Sigmund Freud,* New York: Basic Books, 1961, pp. 53–55.

markable activity of cocaine months before he published his paper, were able to find the only proper and rational application for cocaine: for local anesthetic use in ophthalmology. Dr. Carl Koller, applying cocaine in eye surgery and obtaining impressive if meager results, rather hurriedly prepared the "Preliminary Publication" which was presented at the Ophthalmological Congress at Heidelberg on September 15, only two months after Freud's paper. Thus the priority for the use of cocaine as a local anesthetic was won by Koller, with little credit given to Freud. The competition for the precedence of this discovery did not end there. Another ophthalmologist, also a colleague of Freud, Dr. Leopold Königstein, tested cocaine on a dog's eye and immediately prepared a paper read at a local medical meeting on October 17. Thus we have the amazing picture of three young physicians who were anxious to exploit the properties of cocaine, known already for many years, for their own ambitions.

While the value of cocaine as a local anesthetic was soon firmly established, Freud continued to search for a possible internal application of this drug. He intimated that cocaine might be useful in seasickness, in hydrophobia to relax the throat, and specifically in the treatment of morphine addiction. He continued to give his friend Fleischl-Marxow ever-increasing doses of cocaine. In April 1885 he delivered a lecture in support of general uses of cocaine in which he declared, "I should unhesitatingly advise cocaine being administered in subcutaneous injections of 0.03 to 0.05 grams per dose and without minding an accumulation of the drug."[2] His enthusiasm for cocaine apparently infected many medical men of that time who followed his steps in using cocaine in various diseases.

Soon, however, Freud was confronted with disastrous reality.

[2] *Ibid.*, p. 63.

He found that cocaine had to be administered to Fleischl-Marxow in a constantly increasing daily dose in order to be useful to him. By now he was injecting Fleischl-Marxow with one gram per day. Fleischl-Marxow's general condition was fast deteriorating. He often had attacks of fainting with convulsions, severe insomnia, and his behavior became uncontrollable. He manifested all the signs of grave delirium tremens. Only then did Freud realize that cocaine was a dangerous, habit-forming drug. By the middle of 1886 numerous reports were coming out about the dangerous effects of cocaine in morphine addiction. In July 1886 Professor Erlenmeyer, editor of *Centralblatt für Nervenheilkunde,* wrote a critical article about the use of cocaine. A month later he declared cocaine "the third scourge of humanity," and a year later in his book *Morphia Addiction,* he stated: "He [Freud] recommended unreservedly the employment of cocaine in the treatment of morphinism."

Freud never admitted publicly that his conduct in the cocaine case was hardly ethical or scientific. Many medical men considered his promotion of cocaine as reckless. He met their criticism with an attempt to justify his position. He published a paper in the July 9, 1887, issue of *Wiener Medizinische Wochenschrift* in which he stated that the habit-forming property of cocaine was due not to its toxic effect, but to some patients' predisposition to it. He restated that cocaine given orally is harmless but might be dangerous if injected. He insisted that he had never advocated the use of cocaine injections of Fleischl-Marxow—only the oral use—a statement which simply was not true.

Discussing the cocaine episode, Ernest Jones made a striking statement: "His [Freud's] great strength, though sometimes also his weakness, was the quite extraordinary respect he had for *singular fact.* This is surely a very rare quality. In scientific work, people continually dismiss a single observation when it does not appear to have any connection with other data or general knowledge." And we may add: with carefully conducted experiments.

We may enlarge this statement of Jones. The cocaine episode, as well as many others of Freud's publications and statements, indicates the extreme egocentrism of his character. Almost every self-observation, every fact which he experienced himself, he tended to consider as a general phenomenon, applicable to other men. He had an extraordinary belief, even a conviction that what he found in himself should be present in and experienced by man in general.

"When Freud found in himself," Jones continued, "previously unknown attitudes towards his parents, he felt immediately that they were not peculiar to himself only and that he had discovered something about human nature in general: Oedipus, Hamlet and the rest soon flashed across his mind." His tortuous sexual obsession, particularly when he was engaged to Martha, served as a basis for his theory of neurosis as caused by sexuality.

The case history of Dr. Sigmund Freud has never been fully analyzed. Yet it is essentially an extraordinary one, not dissimilar to that of Auguste Comte, philosopher and the creator of positivism.[3] In his positive philosophy, which made him famous, Comte expressed his belief in the supremacy of the intellect. He proclaimed proudly and unhesitatingly that "The Intellect is my Lord." In his voluminous treatise there was no room for any emotion or sentiment or religion. He was atheistic. Logic based on mathematics, his beloved field of science,

[3]André Cresson, *Auguste Comte: Sa Vi, Son Oeuvre,* Paris: Presses Universitaires de France, 1947; Pierre Ducasse, *Methods et Intuition chez Auguste Comte,* Paris: Presses Universitaires de France, 1939. Boris Sokoloff, *The "Mad" Philosopher: Auguste Comte,* New York: Vantage Press, 1961.

and reasoning along mathematical patterns were the guiding rules which Comte applied with perfection in creating his monumental work. While admitting sociology and history to the select groups of science, in spite of all their scientific imperfections, Comte rejected psychology as a worthless discipline, together with metaphysics and religion. Not only did he proclaim the intellect as the Supreme Power, but he also believed his own intellect was superior to other men's minds.

Nevertheless, at the age of 46, this super-intellectual man rejected all that he had taught and defended for more than two decades. He declared a new social philosophy with the emotions as its basis. He dethroned the intellect and replaced it with a humanitarian religion. His new religion was not based on science. It was not even a vitalistic theory. It was a philosophical concept of the Supreme Power. It was actually a mystical revelation, a beautiful poetic image of the Great Being: the Great Being as Humanity as a Whole, embracing all human beings who have lived and died, who are still living and who will be born in the future. It was a fantastic yet impressive idea of humanity united from its birth through the intimate and spiritual interaction of the past on the present and on the future. This concept denied the death of human individuals. All of them are alive, spiritual partners, infinitesimal molecules in the never-ending chain of human beings. The conduct, the behavior, the creative activity of existing generations of man, or of the men to come, are influenced by all that was done, all that was created by those whose physical existence on earth was terminated yesterday, or a century ago, or even many thousands of years before the man of today was born. In the light of this metaphysical concept one can better understand Comte's famous motto: "The dead govern more and more those who are alive."

This incredible rejection of his original concept by the man who had dominated the positivistic movement in Europe for many decades, was caused by his emotional involvement, by his love for Clotilde de Vaux, whom he knew for only a few short months before she died. But the dead Clotilde remained alive in Comte's imagination for 12 years, until his own death.

The similarity between Freud and Comte ends here. Comte was a born scientist, a mathematician par excellence, who for the great part of his activity adhered to the rules of exact science. This is not true in the case of Freud. As we shall show, he was not, either by his inclinations or his temperament, a scientist in the strict sense of this word, even though he had been trained in exact science and he remained in scientific fields up to the age of 38.

As a faithful student of Dr. Brücke, famous physiologist of Vienna University, Freud started as a biologist, working during the summer at the Zoological Station in Trieste studying the gonadic structure of the eel. At the suggestion of Dr. Brücke, Freud investigated certain cells in the spinal cord of the amoecetes, a primitive fish, and found that these cells were actually spinal ganglion unipolar cells. Not a striking but a well-elaborated undergraduate piece of work. Next, Freud investigated the nerve cells of crayfish—a purely anatomical study. In connection with his histological study, he developed a new technique, the use of gold chloride in staining nerve tissue. Here again his work was of a morphological and not of an experimental nature. In 1881 he was graduated from medical school having to his credit three minor histological papers. A year later Freud decided to leave Brücke's department and to start private practice. As he said on several occasions, he would have preferred to remain a laboratory investigator. "Neither at that time, nor indeed in my later life, did I feel any particular predilection for the career of a physician."[4] At the end of his

4Jones, *op. cit.*, p. 22.

life he acknowledged that: "After 41 years of medical activity, my self-knowledge tells me that I have never really been a doctor in the proper sense. I became a doctor through being compelled to deviate from my original purpose; and the triumph of my life lies in my having, after a long and round-about journey, found my way back to my earliest path. I have no knowledge of having had in my early years any craving to help suffering humanity. My innate sadistic disposition was not a very strong one, so that I had no need to develop this one of its derivatives. Nor did I ever play the 'doctor game'; my infantile curiosity evidently chose other paths. In my youth I felt an overpowering need to understand something of the riddles of the world in which we live and perhaps even to contribute something to their solution. The most hopeful means of achieving this end seemed to be to enroll myself in the medical faculty; but even then I experimented—unsuccessfully—with zoology and chemistry, till at last, under the influence of Brücke, the greatest authority who affected me more than any other in my whole life, I settled down to physiology."[5]

Freud was unable to make a living as a laboratory assistant, particularly because of his intense desire to marry his fiancée, Martha Bernays. He willingly admitted more than once that material success was important to him. He stressed on several occasions that his lack of genuine medical temperament was not greatly to the advantage of his patients and that his interest in patients was that of an experimenter. To a considerable degree his patients served him as human guinea pigs.

Freud's eventual decision to practice medicine and to abandon his research activity was again due to the influence of his professor, Dr. Ernst Brücke. It was Brücke who told him to go into practical medicine. The reason for such unusual advice was

[5]Sigmund Freud, *Autobiography,* New York: Norton, 1935, p. 37.

never fully explained. Possibly Dr. Brücke, an observant man, felt that his student had too much imagination for an investigator in exact science. For three years Freud took training at the Vienna General Hospital, shifting from surgery to dermatology, from psychiatry to nervous diseases, missing pediatrics and gynecology.

It was not easy for a young physician to start a medical practice in Vienna at that time. So Freud decided to seek the professional scientific title of *Privatdocent,* a title which in Austria and Germany indicates a "learned physician." He appealed to his chief, Dr. Brücke, who wrote a flattering comment of his histopathological work to the medical school faculty. The faculty responded favorably and he was nominated *Privatdocent* in neuropathology on July 18, 1885. Soon, again on the friendly recommendation of Dr. Brücke, he received a grant for postgraduate study at Dr. Charcot's Salpetriére Hospital in Paris, where, however, he stayed only four months.

Before he left the Vienna General Hospital, Freud began a histological study on the *medulla oblongata,* and was able to collect some material on this subject. He published three papers, all concerning the acoustic nerve, one of which appeared in *Neurologisches Centralblatt* (June 9, 1885).

Returning to Vienna, Freud for the next five years was absorbed in his private practice, attending also the Neurological Department of Kassowitz's Institute for Children's Diseases. In 1891 Freud published a critical study on aphasia, or impairment of speech. This was not a work based on his own observations. It was a brilliantly written criticism of Wernicke-Lichtheim's theories, as well as those developed by his own professor, Dr. Theodor Meynert. He also offered his own theory of the functional factors involved in aphasia, introducing the new terms of *asymbolic aphasia* and *agnosia* for various types of this affliction. In this book Freud plunged deeply into psychiatric discussion and conclusions, departing to some extent from strictly scientific neurological postulates based on facts and observations. Although this book was recognized as a fine piece of critical analysis, it was not considered by the scientific world as a scientific treatise and was not included in the bibliographies on aphasia.

Freud's private medical practice was not very successful in the beginning, as long as he was treating all sorts of ailments. He apparently did not enjoy this very much but accepted it as the only means for making a living. From his letters one may see that he felt little confidence in his medical abilities and often complained of his sense of inadequacy in dealing with patients. He particularly was not sure of himself when obliged to do minor surgery. He tells us of his unsuccessful minor operation on a well-known actor, Hugo Thimig. The actor never came back to his office. At this time Freud still remained faithful to his training and to the principles of exact science, and considered himself as a neuropathologist dealing with and concerned with scientific facts and observations. But his intimate friendship with Dr. Wilhelm Fliess, who seemed to have had a strong influence on Freud, alienated him gradually from his scientific past.

In spite of his very brief period of association with Charcot, Freud, returning to Vienna, immediately started with his usual enthusiasm to promote hypnotism. On May 11, 1886, he presented a report on hypnotism at the Physiological Club and about two weeks later, on May 27, at the Psychiatric Society. These papers, always cleverly prepared, were received by his colleagues with reservation. Four months later, on October 15, he appeared before the Psychiatric Society with a paper concerning "The Male Hysteria," based chiefly, if not exclusively, on Charcot's work. On the basis of one observation at Salpetriére, a case of traumatic hysteria induced by a fall from a railroad platform, Freud made far-reaching claims about the origin of hysteria in males. This paper was severely criticized as offering nothing new to medical science.

Generally speaking, we are confronted with Freud's peculiar tendency to present medical papers, often prematurely, without previously collecting sufficient scientific evidence of his own. As a result of this last paper, Dr. Meynert excluded him from his department. Freud continued to promote hypnotism for another three years and used it in his private practice, although he admitted that he was often unable to induce a hypnotic state in some of his patients.

Dr. Fliess arrived in Vienna from Berlin in 1887, at the time when Freud was still involved in his work on hypnotism. Two years younger than Freud, Fliess had a good physiological background besides an interest in mathematics. Specializing in the field of nasal and throat infections, a rather narrow field of medical science, he tried to extend his investigations far outside of it. Even though capable, Fliess was apt to inject into his physiological studies a good deal of speculation and conjecture, strongly believing in the power and rightness of his rich imagination. No wonder there was a mutual affinity between Freud and himself. It was Fliess who introduced the new syndrome, the nasal reflex neurosis, which he based on the assumption that there is a relationship between the mucous membrane of the nose and sexual activity. He was never able to prove this; nevertheless he extended his theory to a much wider field, stressing the influence of sexual activity on various processes in the human body and in man's behavior. Fliess's theory apparently gave stimulus to Freud's ideas of a sexual basis of neurosis.

Freud met Fliess in October 1887 and gradually they established an intimate friendship, often discussing problems and theories in which both of them were interested. Commenting on

Freud's friendship with Fliess, Jones writes: "We come here to the only really extraordinary experience in Freud's life. . . . For a man of nearly middle age . . . to cherish a passionate friendship for someone intellectually his inferior and for him to subordinate for several years his judgment and opinions to those of that man: this is unusual, though not entirely unfamiliar."[6]

It was during the years of his friendship with Fliess that Freud formulated his concept on the role which sexuality plays in hysteria and neurosis. At first his postulates were still based on physiology. In his "Studies on Hysteria," Freud stated that "the sexual instinct is certainly the most powerful source of lasting increases in excitation. . . . It is mostly a matter of ideas and processes belonging to the sexual life. . . . This conclusion implies in itself that sexuality is one of the great components of hysteria." A conservative statement, indeed. Discussing the mechanism of anxiety-neurosis, he indicated that the nature of this phenomenon "is to be sought in the defection of somatic sexual excitation from the psychical field." The influence of his scientific training was still so strong on his thinking that he insisted that anxiety-neuroses are a purely physical reaction and cannot be subjected to psychological analysis. "They must be regarded as direct toxic consequences of disturbed sexual chemical processes." And again, "I was thus led into regarding the neuroses as being without exception disturbances of the sexual function, the so-called 'actual' neuroses being the direct toxic expression of such disturbances, and the psychoneuroses their mental expression. . . . The medical aspect of the matter was, moreover, supported by the fact that sexuality was not something purely mental. It had a somatic side as well, and it was possible to assign special chemical processes to it and to attribute sexual excitement to the presence of some

[6]Jones, *op. cit.*, pp. 188–193.

particular, though at present unknown substances."[7]

From his well-known work in collaboration with Dr. Breuer on what they called the *cathartic theory*, was originated his theory of psychoanalysis, with the omnipotent role of the unconscious in neuroses. Freud's collaboration with Breuer was ended because the latter "preferred what might be called a physiological theory. . . . I, on the other hand was inclined to suspect the existence of an interplay of forces and the operation of intentions and purposes."[8] But, as we see, in his *Interpretation of Dreams*, his departure from a biological background is more evident; it is almost complete. In his letter of February 23, 1898 to Fliess he implied that his study on dreams "takes me deeper into psychology than I intended. All my additions belong to the philosophical side of the work, from the organic-sexual there has been nothing." And in his letter of March 8: "It seems to me that the theory of wish fulfillment gives us only the psychological solution, not the biological—or, better, metapsychical one."

It was during these years, 1892 to 1899, that Freud went through a grave crisis at the end of which the skeleton of the psychoanalytic doctrine was created. The nature of this crisis and the underlying factors responsible for it deserve examination.

Here was a medical research man, trained in exact science. Not only was he not an experimental scientist but chiefly a morphologist–histologist. He was taught that physical factors —the body or the soma—have, must have, an indisputable influence upon our mental activity, on our behavior. Moreover, by his scientific education he belonged to the school of uncompromising materialism which advocated the omnipotence of

---

[7]Freud, *Autobiography*, pp. 43–44.
[8]*Ibid.*, p. 49.

chemical factors in man's disease and health. He tried to follow the road designed and indicated by this concept. But gradually, he departed from the rules of exact science investigation and permitted himself to inject an element of imagination and to base his conclusion and theories on poorly founded and inadequate observations. Still he clung to the pattern of exact science investigation even when he was ready to formulate his theories of dreams, or his free association theory. And then step by step he cut off his connection with exact science and plunged deeply into psychoanalytic theory. What elements in his nature were responsible for such drastic deviations from all that he was trained in and had believed in for so many years? The answer might be found in Freud's personality.

In one of his estimates of his own intellectual character he stated: ". . . I am not really a man of science, not an observer, not an experimenter, and not a thinker. I am nothing but by temperament a conquistador—an adventurer, if you want to translate the word—with the curiosity, the boldness and the tenacity that belong to that type of being."[9]

And again "I have never been able to guide my working of my intellect."[10] Freud admits that he had "very restricted capacities or talents. None at all for the natural sciences; nothing for mathematics; nothing for anything quantitative. But what I have, of a very restricted nature, was probably very intensive." If so, what power of activity did Freud possess? Jones gives a very impressive description of Freud's mode of work. It was far from purely intellectual activity such as we see in the cases of a pure scientific mind, either in biology, or physics or mathematics. It is clear, Jones said, that "he was being moved forward almost entirely by unconscious forces and was very much

[9] *Ibid.*, pp. 77–78.
[10] *Ibid.*, pp. 93–94.

at the mercy of them. He oscillated greatly between moods in which ideas came readily into his mind, when there would be a clear view of the conceptions he was building up." And his biographer stresses that the elements indispensable to proper exact scientific work were absent from Freud's personality. "Above all exactitude, measurement, precision, all these qualities Freud knew he was lacking. He rather spurned exactitude and precise definition as being either wearisome or pedantic; he could never have been a mathematician or physicist or even an expert solver of chess problems." In fact, Freud had an obsessive mind. "It was always hard to get ideas out of Freud's head once they had found a foothold."

Jones tries to explain the contradiction of many statements made by Freud during his "crisis": "However unpalatable the ideas may be to hero-worshippers, the truth has to be stated that Freud did not always possess the serenity and inner sureness so characteristic of him in the years when he was well known. The point has to be put even more forcibly. There is ample evidence that for 10 years or so—roughly comprising the nineties—he suffered from a very considerable psychoneurosis." Apparently Freud himself recognized his condition, as one can judge from his letters of that time. His symptoms were quite pronounced: fear of death, dread of traveling by railroad, severe depressions when he was unable to write or to concentrate, spending his hours, when free from practice, in a sort of mental passivity. It was said that during such periods of depression he would cut open books and look for maps of ancient cities. Paradoxically, it was during these years of his psychoneurosis that Freud did most of his original metapsychical work.

We witness here the fascinating picture of dichotomized drivings in Freud's personality during the 10 years of his crisis. He entered medical school not because of his desire to serve suffering mankind or because of a deep attraction to exact science.

He was never fully satisfied with his laboratory work, which required elements and a disposition he did not possess. Yet he did receive a biological education and it exerted a repressive and restrictive influence upon his unconscious creative forces. For 10 years he tried to liberate himself from the bonds of exact science, going through a period of torment, of search for the inner conflicts which were responsible for his neurosis. Only when he freed himself from the influence of exact science, from the effects of his training, did Freud find himself and the "serenity" that Jones described. He found serenity and peace of mind in metapsychics, in the world of illusionary reasoning.

But even in his doctrine of psychoanalysis there was a good deal of conflict and self-rejection. In the early years of psychoanalysis the all-important concept of Freud's doctrine was the unconscious. Yet as years went by, he demoted the unconscious from its position as the central region of the mind. By then Freud had started to consider the unconscious of lesser importance, of being only a quality of unknown phenomenon. The activity and properties of the unconscious were transferred to the Id. And, as is well known, Freud replaced the distinction between conscious and unconscious by the structural organization of the Id, Ego, and Superego. The aging Freud stated that "our scientific work in psychology will consist in translating unconscious processes into conscious ones, and thus filling in the gaps in conscious perceptions." Freud was ready to admit that what is unconscious is actually unknown.

Reviewing the changes and deviations in his personality, which in a sense paralleled the evolution of Freud's doctrine of psychoanalysis, one feels that, at the end of his life, he tended to return to his background and early training as a disciple of exact science.

Psychoanalysis was Freud's beloved child, his creation. It

was psychoanalysis which made him famous and not his meta-psychological articles and books. Yet in this basic and most important field of his activity he manifested quite an unscientific and even unethical attitude. He defended and promoted lay analysis. In 1923 Dr. Brill, his former ardent follower, wrote an article in the New York *Times* criticizing lay analysis. In October of the same year, he announced at a meeting of the New York Psychoanalytic Society that he had decided to break his relations with Freud if he continued to promote lay analysis. Brill pointed out that many Americans, not only without medical degrees but often without any degree at all, went to Vienna where they were given a sort of training in psychoanalytic technique for a few weeks or less. Returning to America with some sort of certificate, these ignorant men began to practice psychoanalysis. Under the advice and efforts of Dr. Brill, the New York state legislature voted a bill, declaring lay analysis to be illegal. This was followed immediately by the decision of the American Medical Association which warned the medical profession against any cooperation with lay analysts. Freud was furious at the American attitude toward lay analysts and published a small booklet entitled *The Question of Lay Analysis.*[11] It was not a scientific defense of lay analysis. It was a popular discussion which he should never have written or published. But Freud wanted to penetrate into America. Indeed, he had once boasted that he would conquer America, and he considered lay analysis a much more effective method for the promotion of his ideas than working through the medical psychoanalysts, who were very few at that time. With Freud's approval, lay analysis flourished in spite of the fact that the New York Psychoanalytic Society passed a resolution in May 1927 condemning lay analysis outright.

[11]London: Imago Publishing Co., 1948.

Jones[12] wrote that "in the late 1930's, a report was widely current in the United States to the effect that Freud had radically changed the views he had expressed so definitely in his brochure on lay analysis, and that now in his opinion the practice of psychoanalysis should be strictly confined in all countries to members of the medical profession." Here is Freud's answer in 1938 to an inquiry about that report: "I cannot imagine how that silly rumor of my having changed my views about the problem of lay analysis may have originated. The fact is, I have never repudiated these views and I insist on them even more intensely than before, in the face of the obvious American tendency to turn psychoanalysis into a mere house-maid of Psychiatry."

Sigmund Freud never changed his position in regard to lay analysis. He defended it stubbornly even at the risk of losing the support of leading medical men practicing psychoanalysis.

It has often been said by Freud's followers and admirers that he was a great scientist, one of the greatest of this century. The objective evidence supplied by himself and by his biographer, Ernest Jones, hardly gives a basis for such an exaggerated statement. Freud was not a great scientist. He was not a genius in any respect. He was not a great philosopher, but, dynamic man that he was, he had extraordinary ability to create metapsychical theories and images which caught public attention. Yet he was a realistic and practical man, especially in the successful promotion of his own teachings.

[12]Jones, *op. cit.,* p. 470.

4

•

Freud and the Human Race: His Ethics

• •

THE psychoanalytic writers, by delving into Freudian meta-psychology and philosophy and complicating it by their dialec-tic discussions, have made it almost impossible for a layman to comprehend the most important question of this teaching: What was the attitude of Freud toward man and toward the human race? From the previous chapter, we learned that Freud, according to his own admission, was not interested in helping patients as a physician, and he was not motivated in his activity by any humanitarian feelings. He was not an idealist as were many medical men, such as Pasteur or Banting. There was no compassion or love or sympathy for suffering mankind in his ideas and writings. His attitude was fully and unreservedly a negative one.

Freud—an Atheist

"He grew up devoid of any belief in a God or immortality, and does not appear ever to have felt the need of it."[1] He disliked Christian beliefs. "There is no reason to think that Freud ever cudgeled his brains about the purpose of the universe—he was always an unrepentant atheist."[2]

A person may be an atheist or agnostic, as many intellectuals are. But most often he remains tolerant toward those who believe in God or a Supreme Power. Not Freud. Like Lenin, he aggressively attacked religion in several of his books, trying to annihilate religion, any religion.[3] He simplified this complex problem, as he did many other problems that he postulated. He stated that natural science denied religion. *This is hardly the truth.* Science is impartial in this respect and many scientists are profound believers. And Freud argued that "the whole thing [religion] is so patently infantile, so incongruous with reality it is painful to think that the great majority of mortals will never be able to rise above this view of life."[4] And again: "If we turn again to religious doctrines, we may reiterate that they are all illusions, they do not admit of proof, and no one can be compelled to consider them as true or to believe in them. Some of them are so improbable, so very incompatible with everything we have laboriously discovered about the reality of the world, that we may compare them . . . to delusion."[5]

For Freud, religion has its origin in man's helplessness. Religion is an illusion which originates in man's individual experi-

[1]Ernest Jones, *The Life and Work of Sigmund Freud,* New York: Basic Books, 1961, pp. 16–17.
[2]*Ibid.,* p. 23.
[3]Sigmund Freud, *Totem and Taboo,* translated by A. A. Brill, New York: 1927; *Moses and Monotheism,* London: Hogarth Press, 1939.
[4]Sigmund Freud, *Civilization and Its Discontents.* London: Hogarth Press, 1929, p. 27.
[5]Sigmund Freud, *The Future of an Illusion,* New York: Liveright Co., 1955, p. 55.

ence as a child. "Being confronted with dangerous, uncontrollable, and not understandable forces within and outside of himself, man remembers, as it were, and regresses to an experience
he had as a child, when he felt protected by a father, whose love
and protection he could win by obeying his commands and
avoiding transgression of his prohibitions.[6] In his turn, Erich
Fromm stresses that to Freud religion was a danger because it
tends to sanctify bad human institutions.[7]

Psychoanalysis views religion both as a neurosis and as an
attempt, within the neuroses of religion itself, to increase consciousness and effect a cure. Psychoanalysis is superficially in-
terpreted as dismissing *religion as an erroneous system of
wishful thinking.* In *The Future of an Illusion,* Freud does
speak of religion as a "substitute-gratification"—the Freudian
analogue to the Marxian formula, "opiate of the people."[8]

In connection with his atheistic credo one may mention that
Freud was very sensitive about his age and that he feared death.
Jones tells us that when Freud was 53, Dr. James Putnam wrote
a favorable article about a lecture Freud had delivered, mentioning, however, that Freud was "no longer a young man."
This hurt Freud a good deal, remarked Jones. Freud wrote to
Jones: "You are young, and I already envy your restless activity. As for myself, the phrase in Putnam's essay, 'He is no
longer a young man' wounded me more than all the rest pleased
me."[9]

During the years 1897–1900, Freud, in his early 40's at that
time, was affected with a sort of anxiety hysteria. "It consisted,"
according to Jones, "essentially in extreme changes of mood

    [6] *Ibid.,* p. 47.
    [7] Erich Fromm, *Psychoanalysis and Religion,* New Haven: Yale University Press,
1964, p. 56.
    [8] Norman Brown, *Life Against Death: The Psychoanalytic Meaning of History,* Mid-
dletown, Conn.: Wesleyan University Press, 1959, p. 13.
    [9] Jones, *op. cit.,* p. 277.

and the only respects in which the anxiety got localized were occasional attacks of dread of dying."[10] It was about that time that Freud was obsessed with fear that he would die before reaching the age of 51. As Freud became older, the thoughts of approaching old age disturbed him a good deal. When he was 59 and still in good health, he again superstitiously believed he had only a year to live. Yet he remained alive another twenty-four years. This terror of death, which often was uncontrollable, reflected more than anything else the inner conflict to his atheistic attitude. And denying God or a Supreme Power, Freud also rejected any possibility of man's immortality, including his own immortality. He was confronted with the fact that when he died there would be only nothingness. And this he was unable to accept. For other men, for humanity at large, the nothingness after death was logical. But not for himself. Here was the tragedy of the self-centered and egocentric Freud.

Death was an obsession with Freud, an obsession more powerful than the Freudians are willing to admit. It influenced his philosophy to a great degree. Thus he devoted a full article to the question of death.[11] He admitted that the psychoanalytic school (meaning himself) could venture on the assertion that at bottom no one believes in his own death, or to put the same thing in another way, in the unconscious every one of us is convinced of his own immortality.[12] And he stressed that "our unconscious does not believe in its own death; it behaves as if immortal."[13] But since Freud, or his conscious mind, did not believe in God or a Supreme Power, or in the immortality of man, he rejected the feeling of his unconscious. Here we have

---

[10] *Ibid.*, pp. 198, 202.
[11] Sigmund Freud, "Our Attitude Towards Death" in Thoughts for the Times on War and Death, Hogarth Press, 1953, p.15.
[12] *Ibid.*, p. 15.
[13] *Ibid.*, p. 21.

a most intriguing interpretation of Freud's inner conflict.

As if expressing his own feeling, Freud declared that "the goal of life is death," and that the death instinct is the most powerful of all in man's existence. Freud reasoned that an organism dies for internal causes, that death is no external accident, and that death is an intrinsic part of life. Freud does not stop here. He emphasized the presence of an aggression instinct in man, which may lead to man's self-destruction. It is, in the words of Freud, a "primary masochism," which he identified with the death instinct. The preoccupation with the problem of death brought Freud, at the end of his life, to the morbid conclusion that life and death instincts are not in conflict, but are, biologically speaking, the same thing. This extreme pessimism of Freud's, hardly known to the public at large, left a strong impact on all his postulates and reflected on his metapsychology.

Purposelessness of Human Existence

Freud refused to believe that there is a purposefulness in man's existence on the earth. To Freud, the appearance of man, or the human race, was an accidental, meaningless event. Man lives only to die. Man is born for no apparent reason. He must suffer. There is no end to his suffering and pain. It is a hopeless, tragic situation.

According to Freud, there was no purpose or goal in the spiritual evolution of the human race, no guideline according to which man evolved from prehistoric man to our present-day *homo sapiens*. This basic question of man's existence was answered by Freud: "One can hardly go wrong in concluding that the idea of a purpose in life stands and fails with the religious system."[14] To an atheist, the answer can be only negative.

---

[14]Freud, *Civilization and Its Discontents*, p. 28.

The Pleasure-Principle

The world is miserable with the instincts of life and death so closely and firmly bound together. Freud continued his pessimistic discussion: "Our possibilities of happiness are limited from the start by our very constitution. It is much less difficult to be unhappy. . . ." Yet the most essential motivating factor in human existence is the pleasure desire. "Our entire psychical activity is bent upon procuring pleasure and avoiding pain, is automatically regulated by the pleasure-principle."[15] And this pleasure-principle, the essence of man's existence, is in conflict with reality, of course, and this conflict is the cause of repression.

Thus, according to Freud, the human race is motivated chiefly by pleasure. The pleasure-principle is the most essential if not the only essential force in our lives. And this principle demands sexual gratification.

He attempts to compare man with animals. Freud stresses that there is only a quantitative distinction between men and animals due to the peculiar prolongation of infancy in the human species. In the case of man, the prolongation of infancy and the postponement of puberty gives infantile sexuality a longer period in which to mature, and at the same time parental care shelters it from the reality-principle. Under these conditions infantile sexuality achieves a full bloom to which there can be no parellel in other species of animals. Hence there is a conflict in the sexual life of man, as there is not in other animals. In man infantile sexuality is never outgrown.

Freud speculates about the dualism of instincts inbred in human nature. There is an irreconcilable conflict between the pleasure instinct (Eros) and the death instinct driving toward death. In his article, "Analysis Terminable and Intermina-

[15] *Ibid.*, p. 29.

ble,"[16] Freud refers to the eternal struggle of life and death in every organism, producing in every human being the spontaneous tendency to conflict.

Freud stressed again and again the indispensability of sexual gratification for man's happiness. He said "that man, having found by experience that sexual [genital] love afforded him his greatest gratification, so that it became in effect a prototype of all happiness to him, must have been thereby impelled to seek his happiness further along the path of sexual relation to make genital eroticism the central part of his life."[17]

As Freud proceeded to paint the picture of the human race, he plunged into morbid conclusions: "The truth is that men are not gentle, friendly creatures wishing for love, who simply defend themselves if they are attacked, but a powerful measure of desire for aggression has to be reckoned as part of their instinctual endowment."

"Our entire psychical activity is bent upon procuring pleasure and avoiding pain, is automatically regulated by the pleasure-principle," and, as a matter of fact, "it is simply the pleasure-principle which draws up the programme of life's purpose."[18]

The problem of sex was an obsession with Freud. Everything started with sex and ended with it. The motivating force of man's behavior, man's pleasure, his gratification, his happiness was in sex.

In his posthumously published book, Carl Gustav Jung[19] analyzes his former friend, Freud. Jung seems to be perplexed with many of Freud's peculiar ideas. The sexual theory was of

---

[16]Sigmund Freud, *Collected Papers*, London: International Psycho-Analytic Press, 1914–1950.
[17]Freud, *Civilization and Its Discontents*, p. 45.
[18]*Ibid.*, p. 50.
[19]Carl Gustav Jung, *Ma Vie, Souvenirs, Rêves, Pensées,* Paris: Gallimard, 1968.

enormous importance to him, Jung noted. "When he was talking about the sexual theory, there was in him a feeling of pressure, almost of anxiety. In Freud in such instances, there was a strange expression of agitation, which was not easy to decipher. . . .

"I was greatly astonished: sexuality was for him a numinosum," a sacred thing, a sort of religion. In one of his conversations with Freud, in Vienna, Jung vividly remembered the words said to him:

"My dear Jung, promise me to never abandon the sexual theory. It is the most essential. Do you see, we must make a dogma, an impregnable bastion."

Perplexed, Jung asked him: "A bastion? Against what?"

Freud's answer was: occultism, meaning philosophy and parapsychology.

Jung refused to accept the doctrine of sexuality, which Freud elevated to an indisputable dogma. "With him," Jung continued, "sexual libido played the role of a hidden god." In fact, Freud never asked himself why he was under obligation to talk continuously about sexuality. Possibly there was some deep-seated reason in Freud for such an obsessiveness with sex, Jung remarks.

Jones[20] tells us that in one of his letters Freud related that his libido had been aroused toward his mother, between the ages of two years and two and a half, on the occasion of seeing her naked. Much later, he became infatuated with his niece, Pauline. In his dreams, he saw her being raped by John, his nephew, and himself together, and actually they often treated the little girl quite cruelly. No doubt there was some element of erotic component on their part. Freud also described the incident when he deliberately urinated in his parents' bedroom after he

[20]Jones, *op. cit.*, p. 54.

saw his father kissing his mother. He was eight years old at that time. Naturally he was reprimanded by his father, who testily permitted himself the exclamation: "That boy will never amount to anything."

Apparently impressed by his childhood experiences and feelings, Freud gave much attention to the problem of sexuality in children. He rejected the popular view that the sexual instinct is absent in childhood and awakens only in the period of life described as puberty. According to Freud,[21] "there seems no doubt that germs of sexual impulses are already present in the new-born child and that these continue to develop for a time, but are then overtaken by a progressive process of suppression."

He takes thumb-sucking as an example of the sexual manifestations of infancy. "Thumb-sucking appears already in early infancy and continues into maturity, or it may persist all through life. It consists in the rhythmic repetition of a sucking contact by the mouth [or lips]. There is no question of the purpose of this procedure being the taking of nourishment. A portion of the lip itself, the tongue, or any other part of the skin within reach—even the big toe—may be taken as the object upon which this sucking is carried out.[22]

And he makes a generalized statement which is hardly justified. "Many of my women patients who suffer from disturbances of eating, *globus hystericus*, constriction of the throat and vomiting, have indulged energetically in sucking during their childhood."[23]

It is of considerable interest that in a footnote to his discussion of infantile sexuality Freud adds: "When the account which I have given above of infantile sexuality was first pub-

---

[21]Sigmund Freud, *Three Essays on the Theory of Sexuality*, London: Imago Publishing Co., 1952, pp. 51–2.

[22]*Ibid.*, p. 58.

[23]*Ibid.*, p. 61.

lished in 1905, it was founded for the most part on the results of psycho-analytic research upon adults. At that time it was impossible to make full use of direct observation on children: only isolated hints and some valuable pieces of confirmation came from that source. Since then it has become possible to gain direct insight into infantile psychosexuality by the analysis of some cases of neurotic illness during the early years of childhood. It is gratifying to be able to report that direct observation has fully confirmed the conclusions arrived at by psychoanalysis—which is incidentally good evidence of the trustworthiness of that method of research."[24]

This admission that he promoted the theory of infantile sexuality when he had no evidence at his disposal, is quite a distressing fact from a scientific viewpoint.

Freud discussed also at length his theory of "penis envy."[25]

"That the girl recognizes the fact that she lacks a penis, does not mean that she accepts its absence lightly. On the contrary, she clings for a long time to the desire to get something like it, and believes in that possibility for an extraordinary number of years; and even at a time when her knowledge of reality has long since led her to abandon the fulfillment of this desire as being quite unattainable, analysis proves that it still persists in the unconscious. . . . The desire after all to obtain the penis for which she so much longs still persists."

This so-called penis envy, and the Oedipus complex linked with it, were not passing fancies with Freud. He remained unreconstructed to the end. In his last book he wrote, "In females. . .we find that it is the effect of their lack of a penis that drives them into their Oedipus complex."[26]

Further, he points out that: "All women feel that they have

[24] *Ibid.*, p. 60.
[25] *Ibid.*, p. 63.
[26] Freud, *Collected Papers.*

been injured in their infancy and that through no fault of their own they have been slighted and robbed of a part of their body. . . . The girl holds her mother responsible for her lack of a penis, and never forgives her for that deficiency."[27]

In Jung's analysis, he concludes that Freud's preoccupation with sex, his declaration that sex is the *deus ex machina*, has its origin in his own personality. For through all Freudian writings, his lectures and discussions, sex was always the major, unavoidable topic. He considered all dreams saturated with sexual visions, and that babies, children, women and men alike have nothing more valuable and important for their gratification than sexual relations. Not spiritual love, not friendship, not creative activity—only sexual relations are what man exists for. In the opinion of Jung, his former friend Freud was a sexual neurotic.

So gradually the image of the human race, of man as such, as described by Freud, is being formed. It is not a pretty image. Man is endowed with three instincts: the instinct of sexual pleasure or Eros, which is the supreme motivating factor in man's existence; the instinct of aggression; and the death instinct. There is nothing positive in the image of man if we accept the Freudian concept of these three instincts. Man is basically lazy; he seeks erotic pleasure most of all; he has no love for his neighbors; he is basically arrogant and aggressive; he is afraid of death. And the human race composed of such creatures has no future, except self-destruction. Here we arrive at a highly important point of Freudian doctrine: What is the relationship between the individual and the society to which he belongs? This is the crucial approach of sociopolitical significance. It is in this respect that the impact of Freud on this country has been particularly strong.

[27]Freud, *Three Essays on the Theory of Sexuality*, pp. 37, 44.

Repression

Here is Freud's attempt to answer the basic question of his reasoning: Why is man unhappy? As we shall see, Freud is inclined to blame society for the unhappiness of an individual, and subsequently civilization as such.

"One word covers the essence of Freud's philosophy," wrote Norman O. Brown.[28] "That word is 'repression.' The whole edifice of psychoanalysis, Freud said, is based upon the theory of repression." Again and again in his writings, Freud returns to the question of man's repression by the society in which he lives. Repression is the basic factor in man's unhappiness, in his inner conflicts, for society represses the individual, and thus the individual is forced to repress himself.

The whole theory of the unconscious is related to the repression of the individual. "We obtain," Freud wrote, "our theory of the unconscious from the theory of repression." And he argued that "the unconscious is the dynamically unconscious repressed." And it is the repressed unconscious which actually interferes with the everyday normal activity of our conscious mind.

To fully understand the meaning of the repression of an individual exerted by society, one must realize what Freud considers to be the most essential motivating factor in human existence, in fact what man's *raison d'être* is.

According to Freud the pleasure (sexual) instinct is in conflict with reality, and this conflict is the cause of repression. "The whole edifice of psychoanalysis," Freud said, "is based upon the theory of repression."[29] Freud's entire life, remarked Brown, was devoted to the study of the phenomenon he called repression. "The Freudian revolution is that radical revision of traditional theories of human nature and human society which

[28]Norman O. Brown, *Life Against Death. The Psychoanalytic Meaning of History*, Middletown, Conn.: Wesleyan University Press, 1959.
[29]*Basic Writings of Sigmund Freud—History*, p. 939.

becomes necessary if repression is recognized as a fact. In the new Freudian perspective, the essence of society is repression of the individual, and the essence of the individual is repression of himself."[30]

Here we are arriving at the heart of Freud's doctrine, or in fact of his ethics. Man is endowed with overpowering instincts for pleasure, for erotic behavior. It is the essence of his existence, the motivating forces in all his existence. But as a member of the society to which he belongs, he is repressed in his sexual drives by this same society. He is repressed by society in the fulfillment of his unconscious drive for complete gratification of his erotic desires. The conflict is unavoidable, indeed. The repression makes him unhappy, miserable, confused, because he is a sensual creature. And under the impact of society's rules and traditions, he unavoidably imposes suppression on himself. This is not an individual case, Freud asserts. It is a general rule which embraces the whole human race. Freud refuses to admit that his conclusions relate only to some individual cases. He applies them to all—each and every man and woman. Here again we are confronted with a typical tendency of Freud to make general conclusions on the basis of a limited number of observations.

Neurosis

What are the consequences of the conflict between our pleasure-seeking instincts and the repression exerted by our society? The answer given by Freud is very clear: it is neurosis. All men and women are affected by neurosis.

Freud maintains that to go from neurotic symptoms and dreams to a new theory of human nature in general involved no further step at all, because the evidence on which the hypothesis

---

[30]Brown, *op.cit.*, p. 3.

of the repressed unconscious is based entails the conclusion that it is a phenomenon present in all human beings. "The psycho-pathological phenomena of everyday life, although trivial from a practical viewpoint, are theoretically important because they show the intrusion of unconscious intentions into our everyday and supposedly normal behavior."[31]

Thus, according to Freud, we are all neurotic. Brown gives his interpretation of this postulate of Freud.

"Or perhaps we are closer to the Freudian point of view if we give a more paradoxical formulation; the difference between 'neurotic' and 'healthy' is only that the 'healthy' have a socially usual form of neurosis. At any rate, to quote a more technical and cautious formulation of the same theorem, Freud says that from the study of dreams we learn that the neuroses make use of a mechanism already in existence as a normal part of our psychic structure, not of one that is newly created by some morbid disturbance or other."[32]

The universal neurosis of mankind is there. Here is the essence of psychoanalysis. Neurosis is not an occasional aberration; it is not just in other people; it is in all of us, and in all of us all the time.[33]

Freud, discussing the nature of pleasure, desire and repression, is inclined to conclude that, "It is in our unconscious repressed desires that we shall find the essence of our being, the clue to our neurosis (as long as reality is repressive), and the clue to what we might become if reality ceased to repress. [34] The results of Freud's exploration of the unconscious can be sum-

[31]Sigmund Freud, *The Ego and the Id*, London: Hogarth Press, 1927; *Delusion and Dreams*, Boston: Beacon Press, 1936.
[32]Norman O. Brown, *op. cit.*, p. 6.
[33]Sigmund Freud, *Collected Papers II*. London: International Psycho-Analytic Press, 1914–1950.
[34]Freud, S.: *A General Introduction to Psycho-Analysis*. London: Allen and Unwin, 1943, pp. 347–65.

marized in two formulas: Our repressed desires are the desires
we had, *unrepressed*, in childhood; and they are sexual desires.

In analyzing neurotic symptoms and dreams, Freud found
that they invariably contained a nucleus representing a return
or regression to the experiences of early childhood. ". . . It was
therefore natural to infer that the adult, in flight from repressive
reality in dreams and neurosis, *regresses to his own childhood*
because it represents a period of happier days before repression
took place."[35]

Freud also stated that the analysis of neurotic symptoms
invariably led not only to the patient's childhood but also to his
sexual life. The symptom is not chiefly a substitute for a pleasure denied by reality, but more specifically a substitute for
sexual satisfaction denied by reality.[36]

Not all psychoanalysts agree with Freud that all men are
neurotic and that their neuroses are closely related to their
sexual-pleasure instinct.

Karen Horney, a well known psychoanalyst stated: "While
I agree that the conflict between individual strivings and social
pressure is an indispensable condition for every neurosis, I do
not believe it is a sufficent condition. The clash between individual desires and social requirements does not necessarily bring
about neuroses, but may just as well lead to factual restrictions
in life, that is, to the simple suppression or repression of desires
or, in most general terms, to factual suffering. A neurosis is
brought about only if this conflict generates anxiety and if the
attempts to allay anxiety lead in turn to defensive tendencies
which, although equally imperative, are nevertheless incompatible with one another."[37]

Much more specific was Carl Gustav Jung who, together

[35]Norman Brown, *op. cit.*, p. 23. (Italics are mine.)
[36]Freud, *Collected Papers.*
[37]Karen Horney, *The Neurotic Personality of Our Time.* New York: Norton, 1937.

with Freud and Adler, was the founder of psychoanalysis. In his autobiography, Jung[38] stated that neurosis may occur without any connection with sexuality, and in fact does occur in such a fashion. The difference in his approach to sexuality and neurosis from that of Freud was the initial cause of his breaking off his relationship with Freud. But the most important factor, in his decision to reject Freudianism, was his religious feeling. He was unable to accept the aggressive atheism of his former friend.

Jung, the son of a minister in Basle, Switzerland, had a vision when he was 11 years old. For three days he had a feeling of growing tension. He was displeased with himself, confused. He experienced fantasies, unable to sleep or rest. Finally he found the courage to face himself and at that moment he saw God in the sky above the cathedral of Basle. This vision never left him. He was never able to accept Freud's cynical attitude toward religion.

Much later, in 1944, he had a strange dream. He arrived at a small chapel near the road. The door was open and he entered. There was neither the statue of the Virgin nor a crucifix. Instead, on the floor there was a figure of a yogi in profound meditation. When he approached closer to the yogi, he recognized himself in him. Jung concluded that this world is nothing but an illusion, an irreality, as the Hindus believe. The true world is the spiritual world and not the material world in which we live.

It is difficult to visualize two persons more different than Sigmund Freud and Carl Jung.

[38]Jung, *op. cit.*

Heredity and Environment

Going through the masses of books, essays, and articles written by Freud, all about man and his psychology, his aberrations, his abnormality and behavior, one is unable to find any reference to the most important factor which made man what he is: *heredity.* All the immense work of genetics is discarded lightly by Freud as if nonexistent. This seems hardly credible. Man is a product of his heredity, and Freud, as a medical man, should have known better. Instead of hereditary factors, the whole doctrine of Freud overemphasizes the powerful influence of environmental factors. His theory of repression is based on his acceptance and promotion of the impact of the surrounding world on man. Yet as biologist–geneticists have proved and demonstrated by endless investigations, the human race, its developmental progress, is insignificantly influenced by environmental forces of whatever nature they might be.

Freud's refusal to admit the magnitude of the role of hereditary characteristics in man's behavior was never brought to the attention of the public at large by his followers, yet his negative attitude in this respect has exerted an enormous influence on the sociopolitical trends in this country.

Freud's doctrines, and particularly his ethics, are the product of his concept of the human race. There is no purpose in man's existence. There is no goal in mankind's presence on the earth. There is no God or Supreme Power. And if this is so, "all is permitted," as Russian nihilists of a century ago declared. Thus the ground for extreme permissiveness is firmly planted by Freud. Man is born only to die. He must profit while he lives. His life is dominated by a pleasure-sexual instinct. Man wants only pleasure; he avoids pain. He does not like to work, because it is society or a nation which represses his instinctual driving, and by doing so makes him miserable and unhappy, inducing neurosis. All men are neurotic. The human race is neurotic. The fault is that of society, or what we might call "The Establishment." The future of the human race is dark, because culture and civilization bring about an ever-increasing and overpowering neurosis. And since society or The Establishment is fully responsible for the misery of man, the individual has no obligation toward society. It is society which must take care of the individual, for he is the victim of The Establishment. Freud actually calls for breaking the bondage imposed by society on the individual.

Freud has a very low opinion of man. Men are cruel, aggressive. They have no love for anyone except themselves. They are erotic and their happiness consists in receiving the greatest possible gratification from intensive sexual intercourse. In brief that is the summary of Freudian ethics, which are accepted, promoted, and applauded by many intellectuals as the basis of the Freudian revolution.

5
.

The Rebuttal of Freud's Ethics

• •

THE tragedy of Freud was his complete rejection, after he reached the age of 45, of biological science in which he had been educated and trained. Instead he became involved in metapsychology, in speculative theories without supporting them by careful and scientific evidence. He built his doctrine on sand, a house of cards, a product of his own rich imagination.

It is our purpose to demonstrate from a strictly scientific viewpoint, the baselessness of many of his postulates.

Man as a Biological Entity

FREUD: *The human race is heading toward self-destruction with its aggression instinct.*

What is man, biologically speaking? Man is a conglomeration of thousands upon thousands of hereditary traces. The individuality of man is enormous in this respect, because he, the individual, is a product of endless generations of the past. The assertion by sociologists, or by men ignorant in biological science, that all men are equal, biologically speaking, is a false scientific conclusion. All men must be equal before the law, but not before Nature.

Fingerprints are the best illustration of the enormousness of hereditary differences in men. Among the billions of men living on the earth at present, none has fingerprints identical with another.

True enough, it is often claimed that environmental conditions are of great significance in affecting the personality of man and are major factors in forming it. However, the fact is that they have no impact on hereditary characteristics, except when their influence extends over many thousands of years. All in all, there is no question that physical heredity is an omnipowerful factor in what an individual is. And this biological axiom is often forgotten or discarded lightly by our psychologists. Behind each of us, there are no less than 100,000 generations of our ancestors, and each of them contributes to our individual characteristics. But whether the Piltdown or Peking man was actually the ancestor of the Neanderthal man, the fact remains that we, each of us, inherited many atavistic characteristics from them, characteristics which were essential for their survival and which are useless and harmful to modern man, such as the appendix, a too-long colon, or some vertebrae.

As there are atavistic organs which occasionally give man trouble, so there are also some physiological manifestations which definitely belong to man's distant past, when they were useful to him. And these structural hereditary characteristics reflect on man's psychology and behavior. Such manifestations as anger, violence, or excessive fear, are atavistic reflexes which contribute greatly to the unhappiness of modern man. Certain inherited structural alterations in our hormonal system, specifically in the adrenal and pituitary glands, are nothing but relics of our past. They—these structural alterations—are responsible for what we may call negative drivings which ferment aggression, violence and cruelty. Thus we agree with Freud that there is an aggression instinct in man. But we disagree that it is a part of the personality of all men.

In many men, in some tribes, some races, some nations, it is almost absent. The great majority of individuals in our civilized society have no tendency, so to speak, for violence, neither in a hidden form nor openly pronounced. Nevertheless, there are individuals in every society, or nation, or tribe who are not only aggressive, or overly aggressive, but are inclined to be violent with little provocation. From a biological point of view the human race, in this respect, is composed of two distinct parts: the great majority and the small minority. The minority of men are endowed with pronounced aggressiveness, which is an atavistic relic of man's past. It is this minority which causes troubles in various places on the earth, by inciting murderous revolts, violence, and bloody wars. Psychophysiologically speaking, there is considerable difference between these two types of men —a difference based on the degree of their atavistic characteristics.

There is overwhelming evidence to the effect that there are in human nature positive, powerful drivings. These positive tendencies—which are manifested in everyday life by the emotions of love, of friendship, of cooperation, and of generosity— are closely interwoven with man's creative activity. Life as the sum total of vital forces, life as an urge for harmony, is represented in man by his positive tendencies and drivings, all of them together striving not merely to preserve harmony in the human organism, but also to make possible a maximum of creative activity. For this reason man instinctively craves an ideology which will give him the possibility for the fullest realization of his positive tendencies.

It is true that the aggressive minority, embodied with atavistic negative stirrings, renders the life of mankind full of misery and unhappiness. But the human race is still in its infancy, as far as psychical evolution is concerned. Man still belongs both to civilization, with its orderly thought, reasoning, and imagination, its positive tendencies; and to the wilderness of the prehistoric eras, with its violence, aggression, fear and terror, its dark and savage forces, and its impulses toward destruction. These two worlds are engaged in constant and often bitter conflict in the arena of man's mind. This transitory period in the existence of the human race might continue for many thousands of years, but the pathways of psychical development are clear: a gradual elimination of atavistic drivings and reactions in human nature. There is no indication, biologically speaking, that the human race is heading towards self-destruction. On the contrary, all that we know about man points to the final victory of our positive tendencies over our atavistic stirrings.[1]

The Death Instinct

FREUD: *Man is born only to die. The Death Instinct is a part of Life.*

On several occasions I had the unfortunate duty to visit men dying from cancer or some other incurable disease, men suffering from intolerable pain. In all instances, as limited as they

[1]This point of view is fully elaborated in my book *Science and the Purpose of Life,* New York: Creative Age Press, 1950.

were in number, I came across a strange phenomenon. Men who during their long lifetime were openly atheists and skeptical about any form of immortality, at life's end were captured by an irresistable sensation, a conviction that they were immortal, both in body and soul, and that there was some mistake in their dying.

Perhaps the most typical case was a friend of mine, a prominent pathologist, in fact a cancer specialist, who was dying from cancer of the liver. He knew that his days were numbered, but he remained stoically calm and tranquil. During the 40 years of his scientific activity he had professed materialistic concepts. Shortly before his death, I spent several hours with him.

"I know that I am dying," he said, "and I'm prepared for this. I admit that it took some effort on my part to accept this fact unreservedly. My instinct to live was so overpowering. But something went wrong with the acceptance I have of approaching death. True enough, I reasoned that after my death nothing will remain of me. Nothing but ashes. Yet recently a new sensation was born in me. First a violent protest against my materialistic conclusion, my beliefs. No, no," he prevented me from interrupting him, "I'm not afraid of death. I'm too sick a man, carrying on an unbearably painful existence. It would be foolish to be afraid of death. Sick as I am, close as I am to my end, I am seized with the most extraordinary feeling that both my body and my soul are immortal. It is not a self-imposed illusion. It comes from somewhere inside of me. The psychologists would say that my subconscious is talking with me."

This was not an exceptional case. In three other cases of professional men, intellectuals par excellence, nonbelievers, I found the same belief in their own immortality.[2]

---

[2] In reference to Freud's psychology concerning his fear of death, we may mention the discussion on the subject of physical immortality which took place at the *First International Conference on the Scientific Prospects for Physical Immortality*, held in Washington, D.C., in December 1963. Peter Wiles, in his article "On Physical Immor-

Man instinctively refuses to believe in the mortality of his body. As we grow older some mysterious force compels us to believe in the immortality of our bodies against all logic, all reasoning, and the cruel knowledge that everything is mortal and that physical death is the ultimate end of all living beings.

This intense instinctive feeling is partially correlated with our instinct of life, which, in fact, reflects man's belief in his immortality. It is an essentially independent emotion which, as investigations have shown, actually reflects the fundamental forces of living nature. It is precisely in the laws of biology and in the vitality of the organism that its genesis may be traced. For man's instinctive belief in physical immortality is a reflection of the potential deathlessness of living matter.

Every living being is mortal. Everything that has a spark of life must die sooner or later. Such has been the conviction of scientists for centuries. Against this established biological axiom, Jennings of Johns Hopkins University was the first to raise his voice. "Every living unicellular organism is endowed with potential immortality," he announced. "Death is merely the biological limitation of life extension."[3]

After years of his own investigation, and on the basis of many other studies, Jennings was in a position to declare that potential immortality of unicellulars does exist. "Potential immortality is the basis of life. It is this which distinguishes the living from the nonliving."[4]

---

tality," *Survey,* No. 56, July 1965, p. 125, London, stressed that "A man of atheistic persuasion but religious temperament [as Freud was—B.S.] faces two psychological problems among others. First he fears death. . . . Second, he wishes to deify man, since with his particular temperament he must believe in God." Yet Freud rejected physical immortality, which was a source of his constant inner conflict as he was aging. We may remember also what G. K. Chesterson once said: "If a man won't believe in God, he will believe in anything." Such was the case of Freud.

[3] H. S. Jennings, "Age, Death and Conjugation," *Popular Science Monthly,* 80:563, 1912.

[4] H. S. Jennings, *Life and Death.* Boston: The Gorham Press, 1920, p. 62.

Jennings' discovery of the potential immortality of unicellulars and certain other lower animals did not have much influence on most biologists. The fact still remained that, although some animals live longer than others, all of them sooner or later grow old and must die. Old age itself was regarded as a process in which the cells of the animal, as well as of the human organism, participated. It was Leo Loeb of Washington University Medical School who made the first breach in this concept. He took a small piece of cancerous tissue from one mouse and transplanted it onto another mouse. He continued to make these transplantations for many months and years and the cancerous cells continued to live long after the original mouse was dead. As Loeb remarked; "There seemed to be no limit to the continuous life inherent in the propagated cells, inasmuch as the termination of these long continued serial transplantations depended solely upon accidental, unfavorable factors which could be avoided."[5]

In other words, cancerous cells are capable of living endlessly as long as the nutritional environment is favorable for their existence. This fact soon became common knowledge among scientists, and the transplantation of tumors is now a routine practice in every cancer laboratory. Some cancerous tissues have been transplanted for more than 60 years and still are as active and vital as the original tissues. Soon it was demonstrated that potential immortality is inbred not only in cancerous cells but also in normal cells, as well as in various organs such as the heart or liver. As Loeb stated: "It could be shown that cells and tissues of mammalian organisms are potentially immortal."[6]

To Loeb it appeared evident that a potential immortality of the cells of higher animals does exist. "Since it was evident that

[5]Leo Loeb, *The Biological Basis of Individuality,* Charles C. Thomas, 1943, p. 45.
[6]*Ibid.,* p. 50.

tumor cells are merely ordinary tissue cells which could be transformed into tumor cells at will under well-defined experimental conditions," he remarked, "the conclusion was justified that also the normal cells from which the tumor cells were derived, have the potentiality to immortal life."[7]

The recent progress in transplantation of organs—heart, liver, kidney, bones, and others—gives additional confirmation to the postulate that living tissue and organs are potentially immortal. Why then does man die? There is an indication that there is in the animal organism some defect, possibly of an endocrine nature, which in its imperfection is responsible for its deterioration. Recent experimentation with the transplantation of various endocrine glands seems to indicate that there is a possibility, perhaps in the distant future, to achieve physical immortality of man.

As Jacques Maritain so aptly stated: "There is in man a natural, an instinctive knowledge of his immortality. This knowledge is inscribed not in man's intelligence, but rather in his ontological structure; it is rooted not in the principles of reasoning, but in his very substance. . . . When the intellect of a man denies immortality, this man continues living, despite its rational conviction, on the basis of an unconscious and, so to speak, biological assumption of this very immortality—though it is rationally denied."[8]

To conclude: *Freud's postulate that there is a death principle or instinct in man's personality is not based on any scientific evidence. There is a powerful life-preservation instinct which reflects the inbred property of living matter, potential immortality, and this instinct is not identical with Eros, or the pleasure instinct, as Freud declared.*

[7] *Ibid.*, p. 52.

[8] Jacques Maritain, *The Immortality of Man,* Boston: The Garvin Lectures, Beacon Press, 1939.

The Pleasure Instinct

FREUD: *The pleasure instinct, Eros, is the most powerful motivating force in human existence.*

Let us assume that Freud is right and that the pleasure
instinct, which he identifies as the sexual drive, is the most
powerful motivating force in human existence. If so, and if this
instinct had dominated the human race for thousands of years,
where would we be now? Obviously a society, any society or
nation, cannot progress if its members build their daily existence and activity on the pleasure-seeking instinct. The human
race, in such a case, would still be in the embryonic state of
civilization, with all the members of a nation taking life easy,
having sexual intercourse, lying on the beaches and eating ba-
nanas or other fruits and vegetables available to them without
much effort. It might have been a pleasant existence, but there
would be no achievement or progress in any respect. There do
exist some tribes of a primitive nature which follow the pattern
accepted by Freud and which for thousands of years have made
no contributions to the progress of civilization. But even with
these primitive people, the Freudian postulates do not seem to
work.

Let us first examine some species in the animal world. We
find that even in such "sexual" animals as monkeys, the sexual
pleasure drive and preoccupation with intercourse depends on
the presence of other distractions.

The following experiment was conducted by Dr. H. Maniser.
Two rhesus monkeys were placed in a six by six-foot cage, a
small cage for these rather large animals. One was a male and
the other a female of smaller size. The cage was placed in a
room where no one disturbed them. Nothing distracted their
attention. It was recorded that these monkeys had intercourse
20 to 25 times every day. All their attention was concentrated

on their desire. Later on, these two monkeys were transferred to a very large cage, located in a zoo surrounded by other cages with various species of monkeys. The frequency of intercourse went down drastically to one to two times a day. Their attention was now directed to other aspects of their existence: the birds, other monkeys, the visitors. This experiment seems to demonstrate that an artificially induced concentration on sex only increases the sexuality of animals.

Sex in animals takes up only a very small part, hardly more than one percent, of their time. In normal man, with his various interests and drives, sex is an infinitesimal factor, in terms of his time.

It was estimated that a normal healthy man, married, would spend no more than 0.3 percent of his lifetime on his erotic pleasure drive. In fact he spends more time on shaving, bathing, or on meals than on intercourse. There are exceptions, of course. There are some races which prefer pleasure gratification to anything else. There are, as well, individual men and women who are addicted to a pleasure-seeking existence. But the great majority of humans in nations which belong to the progressive civilizations spend the largest part of their lives on creative activity. Retired men, who dreamed of taking life easy while they were still engaged in gainful occupation, once free from the necessity of earning their living, prefer to do some work: gardening, repairing their houses, hobbies, and many other activities which are associated with work. A man who finds himself suddenly in a position to immerse himself in pleasure, sexual or other, soon finds that he is bored to death by doing nothing constructive, that he is eager to work on some project, even an insignificant one.

This basic property of human nature has its origin in the creative instinct. It was this instinct which brought the human race from the wilderness of the jungles to a position where it has gradually conquered the outside world. It is a powerful instinct, much more pronounced than the pleasure-principle, at least in those nations and races which created the present civilization of art, music, science, and industry. Truly enough, there are races which have remained at a level of primitive development due to the absence of or deficiency in their inbred creative instinct.

The creative instinct has its biological background in certain constitutional structures of the living organism. It was Spemann[9] who first induced the term of *organizers* for the creative factors in living organism.

The organizers, which might be primary or secondary depending on their role in developmental processes, may be defined as morphogenic contact substances. They actually serve as tissue transformers or, more precisely, as *inductors*. They cause the tissue with which they come into contact to undergo certain changes. In embryonic tissue which is still undetermined and has, therefore, many *potencies* or *fates*, the organizers may determine which of their potential differentiations the tissues should undergo. Originally the term organizer was used only in the case of embryonic development, but gradually it acquired a more general meaning and is now frequently applied as a designation for the organ-forming substances, including the brain and other parts of the nervous system.[10]

[9]H. Spemann, *Embryonic Development and Induction,* New Haven: Yale University Press, 1938. See also Richard Eakin: "The Nature of the Organizer," *Science, 109*:195, 1949.

[10]There is a hierarchy of organizers, each of which plays its own role in the development of the organism, and in a developed organism, in the formation of new ideas, reflexes, and mental activity. In the process of transformation, the organizer participates in the production of a new organizer or organizers, which in their turn induce certain differentiation in the tissues, organs, and impulses. The organizer acts in association with the inherent characteristic of the tissue. It is the tissue which serves as a substratum, or as an arena, as it were, to the organizer. Therefore the organizer is essentially a part, an innate part, of the inner environment of the tissues. Joseph Needham, *Biochemistry and Morphogenesis,* London: Cambridge University Press,

As the reflection of the presence in man's bodily system of a powerful natural organizer, it appears that there is in a man a principle or an instinct which imposes on him a demand for creative and/or organizing activity. The story of our civilization indicates fully that man possesses such an organizer or creative instinct, and that there is an inner drive in man which renders creative activity a necessity to him. It is a part of our nature, our personality. True enough, the pleasure-seeking tendencies are also present, often interfering with our constructive drives, but they are of secondary significance in the evolution of the human race.

To conclude: *There is no scientific evidence to support Freud's postulate that the "pleasure-principle" or "pleasure-instinct" is the major factor in the existence of the human race. On the other hand, there is in man's organism a principle or instinct of creation or organizing which induces man to seek constructive goals and perform constructive work, and which chiefly has been responsible for the phenomenal progress of our civilization.*

Repression

FREUD: *Society represses the individual, specifically his pleasure-sexual instinct. This induces neurosis in him. All men are neurotic. The human race is neurotic.*

The theory of the repression of an individual by society, as developed by Freud, is of considerable interest. Freud approached this problem exclusively from a speculative psychological premise. He ignored man as a biological entity and the inbred hereditary factors present in the human organism. Discussing this problem, we must first return to the question of the

1942; J. Brachet, *Cold Spring Harbor Symposium, Quantitative Biology* 1947; L. G. Barth and S. Graff, *Cold Spring Harbor Symposium, Quantitative Biology,* 1947.

permissiveness syndrome, which is a part of man's nature. As we pointed out, the child is endowed with an unlimited permissiveness syndrome. As the child grows there appears in him a nucleus of self-control. Even if he is not instructed or restricted by his parents, this self-control gradually takes hold of his permissiveness tendencies and restricts them. The proper education by parents helps to speed this self-control. Yet in some children who are endowed with strongly pronounced permissive tendencies, even parental education encounters difficulties in regulating them. The self-control of a growing child reflects an oncogenic process, coordinated with the development and progress of our civilization, which is a phylogenetic process. As a child grows into a young man, he must naturally adapt himself to the conditions of civilized life, to the rules according to which its existence is regulated. He must take into consideration the rules of the society in which he lives, and these rules must be accepted if he wants to be a useful member of it. But he is not under repression by the society.[11] He is adapting himself to this society. He can reject the rules and remain antisocial. His process of adaptation is of much less significance than the individual's natural self-control.

We find the development of self-control in some species of dogs. Some dogs, some species of dogs, do not need to be housebroken at all. As they grow and mature, they behave perfectly without any training by their masters. They exert remarkable self-control while some other species of dogs lack this self-controlling power in spite of their masters' most energetic efforts.

Unfortunately, there are individuals or even tribes which demonstrate the most peculiar absence of self-control, even

---

[11]E. C. Mitchell and D. W. Goltman, *American Journal of Disturbed Children,* 59:379, 1940.

when strong efforts are made to develop self-control in them.

This developmental process of self-control is closely associated with or parallels the mental and emotional maturity of a child, of a young man, of an adult. One often meets a young man or girl who is immature and manifests the absence of self-control to a considerable degree. They retain the permissive syndrome unabated through their childhood, and often through their adult life. Such individuals are imbued, from a biological viewpoint, with some atavistic trends, relics of mankind's past.

And here we arrive at another biological factor which is present in human nature, as well as in human society or a nation —so-called *homeostasis*. Sociologists and historians, although detached from the biological sciences, long ago recognized the fact that a healthy, properly functioning society or nation possesses a sort of equilibrium. Any deviation either to the left or to the right gradually brings about a tendency to restore the equilibrium of the social entity. A radical movement to the left sooner or later swings to the conservative right, and ultimately the society or the nation takes the middle-road policy, if of course the nation is healthy and vital, a progressive, creative nation. The same picture exists, impressively so, in the human body. And this equilibrium force is called homeostasis.

It was Walter Cannon, the famous Harvard physiologist, who first introduced this term:[12]

"The constant conditions which are maintained in the body," he explained, "might be termed *equilibrium*. That word, however, has come to have fairly exact meaning as applied to relatively simple physicochemcial states, in closed systems, where known forces are balanced. The coordinated physiological processes which maintain most of the steady states in the organism are so complex and so peculiar to living things—that I have

---

[12]Walter B. Cannon, *The Wisdom of the Body*, Norton, 1932.

suggested a special designation for these states, *homeostasis.*"

Not unlike a society, homeostasis in the human organism protects it against all possible physical and mental aberrations. Or rather homeostasis tries to maintain a certain equilibrium which is disturbed by various factors. In infection, with high fever, homeostasis calls for the defense of the organism, mobilizing the white blood cells. When man is angry and his adrenal gland produces excess adrenalin, homeostasis calls for chemical agents which immediately oxidize the adrenalin and destroy it. The psychophysiological role of homeostasis as controlling our atavistic reflexes is of prime importance. It is not a repressive factor, least of all that. Basically, one might consider it as the positive factor in man's existence, which prevents him from extremes in his daily reflexes.

Yet homeostasis is helpless to assist the organism if it is in a dangerous state of aberration, when the human organism is degenerating, either physically or mentally. That is the case when a child or a man is imbued with an extreme permissiveness syndrome. The homeostasis in such cases is partially destroyed and unable to act properly from a psychophysiological view point. Man's entity is lost. Man obsessed by his negative drivings might become neurotic or psychopathic.[13]

This brief excursion into human equilibrium and homeostasis brings us to a confrontation with Freud's postulate that society represses man, making him neurotic. The scientific evidence about homeostasis corresponds to what was said about man's self-control and his atavistic tendencies. The essence of self-control, a psychological term, is the equivalent of homeostasis, biologically speaking.[14]

[13]Leo Loeb, *op. cit.*, and personal discussion with Loeb on the subject of homeostasis.
[14]Norman Brown, Professor of Classics at Wesleyan University—in his *Life Against Death: The Psychoanalytic Meaning of History,* Middletown Conn.: Wesleyan University Press, 1959—misinterpreted the meaning of the term homeostasis, considering it

To conclude: *There is no repression of an individual by society as far as the great majority of normal healthy men are concerned. It is an inbred property of a mature man to develop self-control, a product of homeostasis, a biological regulating factor of human nature. Man tends to adapt himself to the rules of the society of which he is a member. But society represses individuals who are unstable, immature, predisposed to neurosis or psychopathy, and who demonstrate an extreme permissiveness syndrome. Such individuals lack, partially or completely, the self-controlling factor, inbred in human nature and known as homeostasis. The theory of Freud about the role of repression of individuals by society was based on his observations of neurotic patients and not of normal healthy individuals. His generalization of the theory of repression has no foundation, biologically speaking.*

The Purposefulness of Human Existence

FREUD: *There is no purpose, no goal in the existence of the human race. Its appearance on the earth was accidental. There is no Supreme Power which guides the development of the human race or the living world in general.*

Atheists who deny the existence of God base their philosophical concept on so-called materialistic or mechanistic theories of living matter. According to those who reject God and a Supreme Power there are nothing but chemical factors acting at random, in a senseless manner. We are going nowhere, helpless pawns moved around and around by the variety of chemical and physical molecules. Many scientists have protested and fought against this concept, which is promoted aggressively by

---

as a sort of neutral passivity of the organism, while actually this term signifies a mobilization of all natural forces of the living organism.

Marxist materialism, and which was defended vigorously by Freud. There is considerable biological evidence which contradicts the primitive materialism and defends what is called the *neovitalistic theory* which recognizes Supreme Power guidance and which is based on belief in God. Yet the materialistic power is very strong in exact science. J. B. Rhine correctly summarizes the situation: "Whenever science came in, the traditional belief in man's spiritual nature went out. Psychology became increasingly saturated with physical concepts. The physicalistic doctrine of man did progress from a crude materialism to theories patterned after those of modern physics; but the dominance of physical analogy still remains." And he bitterly complains, "There is no tolerance left in the sciences for anything like the nonphysical, or exclusively physical, reality which men once labeled the soul."[15]

Yet many leading scientists are rejecting the materialistic concept. Max Planck, the great scientist–physicist, does not hesitate to say: "Thus we see ourselves governed all through life by a Supreme Power. . . . No one who thinks can ignore this."[16] Lecomte du Noüy, famous physicist and mathematician of great repute, added his voice to the swelling chorus when he announced that the materialistic theory of the universe and of man is no longer tenable.[17]

Nicolas Lossky, noted philosopher and biologist, strongly attacked the materialistically minded biologists: "Why is the natural science of today so hopelessly lost in the technical smallness of biological research? Why is there no attempt, any serious attempt worth speaking about to penetrate the mysteries of living matter? Why are such attempts condemned in advance by our leading men of biology? The answer may be

[15]J. B. Rhine, *The Reach of the Mind,* New York: Sloanes Asso., 1947.
[16]Max Planck, *Scientific Autobiography,* New York: Philosophical Library, 1949.
[17]Pierre Lecomte du Noüy, *Between Knowing and Believing,* New York: David McKay, 1966.

found in the mechanism of our perception. For our natural science is a product of pure intellect."[18]

Neovitalism has built the case against materialistic theories by a series of very complex and highly intriguing biological experiments on various organisms. Thus Hans Driesch, professor of Embryology at Heidelberg University, Germany, demonstrated that it is possible to obtain a complete larva from each of the two blastomeres of the two-cell stage. By this experiment he proved that the original one-cell egg is neither mosaic nor predetermined.[19]

Further experiments along these lines have shown that the original one cell possesses what is called *prospective* potency which is in fact a *pluripotency.* It was demonstrated by numerous experiments on sea-urchin eggs, that the actual fate of an egg cell is only one among many other possible fates. The neovitalist embryologists introduced the term *harmonious equipotential system* as represented by an undetermined cell in which each part is endowed with the same potentiality or potency. It is now generally accepted by biologists that not only at the stage of the egg cell, but up to a certain stage of gastrulation, the fate of most of the embryonic regions is not irrevocably determined. But how is this *determination* brought about? What factors guide or direct the *undetermined* egg cell, and by elimination of various *fates* and *potencies,* lead to a proper differentiation of tissues and organs? Can chemical or physical factors make such a rational choice? Such a possibility seems incredible. The neovitalists believe and actually have demonstrated that only the presence of a nonmaterial force in the living matter can explain this extraordinary phenomenon of

---

[18]Quoted from Boris Sokoloff: *Science and the Purpose of Life. Science versus Materialism,* New York: Creative Age Press, 1950, p. 8.

[19]Hans Driesch, *Biol. Centralbl.,* 47:651, 1927. Also: *The Science and Philosophy of the Organism,* Gifford Lectures, 1928; "Fusion of Two Blastulae of Echinus," *Arch. f. Entwicklgamech., 10*:411, 1926.

embryonic growth. It was Driesch who introduced the term for this factor, marking it at first with the letter E.

"It was not without design," said Driesch, "that I chose the letter E to represent this. Let that factor in life phenomena which we have shown to be a factor of true autonomy be called *entelechy*." What is this entelechy or, as it is often called, the *vis vitalis* of the neovitalistic doctrine? Neovitalists defined this power as intensive manifoldness, which lacks all the characteristics of quantity, and which does not exist in space, but is able to act anytime and anywhere in the living organism. Seemingly it cannot be measured, it does not enter any form of energy, and it is not, therefore, a physical or chemical factor. Essentially it is not a material factor. Yet it is a moving force of embryonic development, a unifying factor of living matter which makes the organism what it is—an individual living unit.

The famous biologist Joseph Needham, an outspoken materialist, is reluctantly willing to admit that "some nonspatial agency, [meaning entelechy] must be acting upon the shuffled blastomeres in a marshalling manner."[20]

In reviewing various experiments conducted by biologists in order to show the presence of a powerful force in the ontogenetic and phylogenetic developments of living organism, I arrived at the conclusion that there is unquestionably a finality in living matter. And I agreed with Planck and other scientists that there is—there should be—a purpose in the existence of the human race and that materialism is in no position to explain the mysterious guidance present in living matter, unless by admitting fully and unreservedly the existence of a Supreme Power, of God.[21]

---

[20]Joseph Needham, *Biochemistry and Morphogenesis.* Charles Thomas, 1935.
[21]Boris Sokoloff, *Science and the Purpose of Life: Science versus Materialism.* New York: Creative Age Press, 1950, pp. 1–284.

Intelligence and Environment

FREUD: *Environmental factors have an overpowering influence on human behavior and personality.*

This is one of the most intriguing questions of modern psychophysiology. Among all the countries of the world, only the United States goes to the extreme in minimizing the role of hereditary factors, and grossly exaggerating the impact of environmental forces on man's personality and intelligence. And yet this country has produced many thousands of men—born in gloomy hopeless poverty and unable to obtain the education which more privileged citizens have received—who achieved greatness. We do not need to go further than to cite the cases of two Presidents, Abraham Lincoln and Andrew Johnson. Their poverty was incredible, infinitely more devasting than what we now call poverty. And yet, in spite of the most discouraging environmental conditions, they reached the highest places in this country. Both men were of extraordinary intelligence—a product of their heredity.

Today it is often said that environmental factors affect man's intelligence, but this has never been proved by any strictly scientific investigation. The I.Q. remains static, with only a slight permanent deviation in healthy, normal individuals, in spite of all favorable or unfavorable external educational influences.

Here again comparative anatomy and neurology show that even before the beginning of the Tertiary Period, the trend had already been determined for that particular line of brain development, and the continuation of this development eventually led to the emergence of man's distinctive attributes which cover what we call intelligence. Moreover, man is the ultimate product of that line of ancestry which was never compelled to turn aside and adopt protective specializations, either of structure or mode of life, which would be fatal to its plasticity and power of further brain development. There was no room in man's brain development for environmental factors. Human races living in various parts of the world, under different physical conditions, show the same pattern of progressive development. The only difference is that some races evolved in regard to their brain structure more slowly than others.[22] Thus, from a biological viewpoint, it appears quite futile to assume or to declare that the inherited basic intelligence of man can be influenced by any educational training, except for some superficial manifestations and behavior.

In his recent survey, Sir Cyril Burt, eminent British educator, was unable to correlate the I.Q.'s of students to their economic status. On the basis of the results he obtained, Burt rejected the claim by sociologists and psychologists that early home life was the clue to intelligence. Children raised in orphanages gave the same figures of intelligence as those from well-to-do families. Burt denied that poverty and poor cultural conditions reflect on man's intelligence, although he admits that environmental factors might have some small impact on the ability to demonstrate intelligence.[23]

Helmut Schoek[24] arrived at similar conclusions. He refers to a social survey, *Social Mobility in Britain.* According to the results of this survey any approximation of "equality of opportunity" is probably more disruptive of human relations than the inequalities of the past and present. Hereditary factors play a major role, with the intelligence of an individual affecting his

[22]One finds much material on this topic in *Problems of Personality. Studies in Honour of Morton Prince.* London: Kegan Paul,
[23]Sir Cyril Burt, *"Irish Journal of Education,"* October 1969.
[24]Helmut Schoek, *Essays on Individuality,* Felix Morley, ed., Philadelphia: University of Pennsylvania Press, 1958.

success or failure in his enterprise. "It seems that only the existence of unequal external opportunities makes it possible for the unsuccessful individual to live with himself. As long as unequal chances are known to exist, failure can be blamed on external conditions, rightly or wrongly. But how can the individual think well of himself if I.Q. tests and personality factors alone have determined his place in society? Social scientists pushing men into unrealistic aspirations to, and beliefs in, irrational 'equal opportunities' may actually produce the frustrated human beings whom they like to explain as victims of the present social system."[25]

One of the most intriguing aspects of the concept of society versus individual is the relationship between intelligence and the permissiveness syndrome. Let us take an example, a very common example indeed, in the American society of today. A boy, in his early youth, 9 or 10 years old, showed considerable intelligence. Yet his parents as well as the school were permissive. They allowed him to do what he wanted to do. He smoked at the age of 13. He took dope at 14. He was in three car accidents, once with a friend who was gravely injured. At 17 he joined the hippies, and soon became one of the militant students. The question is: What became of his I.Q.? Of his intelligence? He claims that he is a revolutionary, and that he defends and promotes a new America. He sincerely believes that he is very intelligent. Yet when a survey was conducted on a group of such young men, including this one, their I.Q.'s, *as well as his,* were quite low, in fact lower than in their youthful years. How would psychophysiologists explain such a phenomenon? Some of them would say that these brains had been affected by narcotics.

[25] *Ibid.,* p. 113.

What is intelligence, from a biological viewpoint?[26] Is intelligence influenced by environmental factors, as the majority of sociologists believe?

Leona E. Tyler cited the results conducted by numerous investigators along these lines: "They furnish no evidence that intelligence is more dependent upon environmental differences than eye color or height is."[27] Jones and Conrad[28] arrived at similar conclusions. Thus psychological studies, intended to establish the role of environmental forces in intelligence, ended in negative conclusions. All these scientific data confirm our statement that intelligence is correlated to brain structure, a product of hereditary characteristics. As such it is highly individualistic. It took hundreds of thousands of years to develop in man the present brain structure related to his intelligence.

It takes about 20 to 25 years for modern individuals to complete the development of their intelligence. There is a "maturity process" in this development. Intelligence is associated with reasoning, the ability of self-direction, which is absent in early childhood and often in older young men and women who remain "immature" in spite of their education. And as indispensable parts of the intelligence activity are the control of our atavistic reflexes and the inbred permissiveness syndrome, which is entirely of an emotional nature.

The decline of intelligence is a well-known manifestation. It can and does occur in the individual who takes narcotics, or

[26]Erich Fromm, *Man for Himself,* New York: Rinehart, 1947, differentiates between intelligence and reason: "Intelligence is man's tool for attaining practical goals with the aim of discovering those aspects of things the knowledge of which is necessary for manipulating them. . . . Reason involves a third dimension, that of depth, which reaches to the essence of things and processes. While reason is not divorced from the practical aims of life, it is not a mere tool for immediate action." P. 102. [A very artificial definition, for reasoning is a part of intelligence—B.S.]

[27]Leona E. Tyler, *The Psychology of Human Differences,* New York: Appleton-Century, 1956, p. 484.

[28]H. F. Jones, and H. S. Conrad, "The Growth and Decline of Intelligence. *General Psychol. Monographs, 13*:223–298, 1933.

who is captivated by permissive drives, or affected by mental aberrations.[29] In the light of our biological knowledge we should approach the so-called revolutionary movement among American youths, their riots, their attraction to narcotics. This movement is not against The Establishment or our social system; it is a protest against their own inbred "intelligence" and reasoning which binds them to self-direction and self-control. This movement is least of all revolutionary, from a biological viewpoint. It is reactionary, a retrograde trend towards the primitivism of the human race, when intelligence and reasoning were at their lowest level, when they were in an embryonic state.[30]

During the evolvement of man's brain structure, which went on for hundreds of thousands of years, there were setbacks due to various factors, some of them genetic, which resulted in a temporary retrogradation of brain structure. Possibly we are now confronted with the same phenomenon which would result in a striking reduction of intelligence in the generation to come, the generation born out of our "revolted" youth, engrossed in narcotics.

To conclude: *Intelligence is a hereditary phenomenon, a product of the brain structure. It is not influenced by environment. It goes through a maturation development in the individual. It is a self-directing and reasoning factor. It can decline or even retrogress under the influence of drugs, and in such cases it loses control over the self-direction syndrome. There is a danger that the children of our "revolted youth" will be bearing a reduced intelligence.*

[29]Frank Falkner, ed., *Human Development,* Philadelphia and London: Saunders, 1966.
[30]*Ibid.*

Man as a Chemical Entity

FREUD: *Society represses individuals, causing neurosis.*

The strongest blow to the Freudian doctrine was delivered by a new science known as psychochemistry. It is a relatively new science, two or three decades old. It offers enormous amounts of data, properly collected and scientifically verified.[31]

For a long time there were indications that neurosis and other mental manifestations could be caused by some changes in the chemistry of the body, without any relationship to surrounding influences. In fact Carl Jung, former associate of Freud, was one of the first to suggest that some substances, called *metabolites,* present in our organism, can be responsible for our mental and emotional alterations. But even before the new science of psychochemistry was born, physicians were often confronted with altered or peculiar behavior of their patients for no detectable reason.

There is the case of a middle-aged man of excellent disposition, an extrovert, who always saw the world in a rosy light and who was, as he admitted, a perfectly happy man. Then quite suddenly he became morose, antisocial. He saw everything around him in a dark light. He was depressed and utterly unhappy. No apparent illness was detected until it was found that his icterus index was very high, meaning that there was an excess of bile in his bloodstream. When the icterus index was brought down to its normal level by a routine treatment he

---

[31]Otherwise known as psychopharmacology. Many books and endless scientific articles were published on this subject, and it is not my intention to cover this field on a large scale. Only a brief sketch is offered to illustrate the pathways of this science. Among the recent books deserving the attention of readers is: Max Rinkel and Herman C. B. Denber, ed., *Chemical Concepts of Psychosis,* New York: McDowell-Obolensky, 1958. There are also several journals devoted to this problem, such as *Psychopharmacology Abstracts,* published by the Department of Health, Education, and Welfare, which gives abstracts of all important discoveries along these lines.

returned to his previous self. He was again a happy, jovial man.[32]

Dr. Henri Baruk, Professor of Experimental Psychiatry and Psychopharmacology at the University of Paris Medical School, reported in numerous publications that many harmful substances present in the human body can induce certain nervous and mental ailments in man. Such a natural substance as bile, when in excess in the human or animal body, might influence the basic aspects of personality and induce neurosis.

Baruk and his associates found that there are two kinds of toxic substances. One group is responsible for causing the state of somnolence and drowsiness, resembling sleep. Animals given these toxic substances are reduced to the status of automatons. They are mentally inert. Volition and spontaneity are reduced, if not absent. They are what we call *catatonic*. The other group of toxic substances present in the body acts differently. They have a stimulating action. They excite the person, who becomes agitated, cannot sleep and talks endlessly. Similar effects were observed when there was an excess in the body production of hormones.[33]

Baruk stated: "Our investigations have led to increased emphasis on a type of disorder characterized by a loss of volition and by regression. This syndrome is the result of a general intoxication originating at some distant organ, such as the intestines, the liver, or the endocrine glands; this general intoxication produces, secondarily, functional disorders of the brain

---

[32]Boris Sokoloff, *The Achievement of Happiness,* New York: Simon & Schuster, 1938.

[33]The French scientists reported an interesting case of a patient who received a colibacillus toxin. "She developed a clear catatonia, becoming immobile, almost resembling a statue. She explained, after her recovery, that she felt as if she were asleep, and in a disagreeable state of listlessness. Afterward, in a dream she imagined herself in an airplane going to Russia where she was to be executed. This delusion seemed to explain her gesturing and postures." H. Baruk, "Origine digestive et Hepato-Intestinale de certaines Maladies Mentales," *Schweiz. med. Wchschr.*, *83*:1317–8, 1953.

leading to changes of the total personality."[34]

Some years ago I was associated with St. Roques Hospital in Nice, France. One afternoon when I was making a tour with my colleague Dr. Volpatti, the police called the hospital. It was an emergency call. A nude woman was walking along the Promenade des Anglais, in the fashionable center of the city, gesticulating and trying to attract the attention of men, even if they were with their wives. We immediately went in an ambulance to the Promenade and found the woman, not far from the Hotel Negresco. Yes, she was nude, completely nude. She was in a state of high excitement, smiling, giggling, trying to talk with men, disregarding women. She was surrounded by a small crowd which was growing steadily. She was about 40, with an excellent figure, slightly overweight. She was not beautiful but she had an attractive face, a distinguished face. Her hair was in disorder, brownish, slightly graying. But her eyes, dilated and inflamed, gave the impression of mental disorder. She did not protest our invitation to follow us, and in almost no time we took her in the ambulance to the psychiatric ward of the hospital. Her speech was confused, and she was unable to tell us her name. Soon, however, an older man arrived at the hospital and informed us that he was Prince Serge, the husband of the woman, Princess Diana. He explained to us that she was going through an acute period of menopause, was apparently mentally diseased. He kept her at home, but she had escaped while he was out.

Prince Serge explained to us that until a few months before, his wife had been a perfectly normal person, of excellent disposition, always tactful and correct in her behavior. And then it started. It started gradually. There were some irregularities in

[34]H. Baruk, "Experimental Catatonia and the Problem of Will and Personality," *Journal of Nervous Mental Disorders, 110*:218–233, 1949.

her menstruation. She was restless, distracted, often talking frivolously. She seemed to be attracted to younger men, and gave much more attention to her appearance than before. As time went on, her condition worsened. She became quarrelsome, complaining, dissatisfied with everything. Now and then she tried to approach strange men, which shocked her husband. He took her to a physician who referred her to a gynecologist. The diagnosis was clear: she was affected with an acute form of menopause. "She is producing an excess of the sex hormone, the so-called estrogenic substance."

"But she is young!" Prince Serge protested. "Hardly forty."

Princess Diana remained in the psychiatric clinic for eight months, kept on sedatives and other more specific medications. She persistently tried to take her clothes off, particularly in the presence of males. In the confused state of mind she was in, she was unable to remember her own name and hardly recognized her husband.

Gradually her condition improved and a year later when I visited them at their home, she was almost her normal self. This was a typical case of sexual neurosis, caused by an excess of estrogenic hormone.

This condition, the neurosis, was not caused by "repression of the individual by society," as Freud postulated. There were no environmental factors involved in this case as there are not in millions of cases of women going through the menopause. In this case internal "chemical factors" were entirely responsible for the emotional disturbances, mental aberrations, and neurosislike manifestations.

About one million women in this country are going through the menopause. There are almost no abnormal manifestations in many of these women. They might be somewhat more excitable, restless, and irritable, with their sexuality increased, but otherwise one cannot detect any neurotic manifestations. On the other hand, there are numerous cases of considerable emotional and mental disturbances in menopausal women. The influence of excessive production of estrogenic hormone can be so acute that some women might become psychotic. And the tragedy of such extreme cases is that originally these women were placid, good-tempered, and mentally and emotionally normal.

The ovarian hormones are not the only chemical factors which can induce neurosis. Dysfunction of the thyroid gland or adrenal gland or other endocrine glands often leads to emotional unbalance and mental aberrations. As Henning Andersen remarks: "From studies of the experiments on human beings, a clearer understanding emerges of the connection between the endocrine glands and the effects of their function— or dysfunction—on man."[35]

Now let us turn our attention to another substance which is naturally present in our organism. It is called serotonin.[36] Fifteen years or so ago, there was very little known about this metabolite. But during the last decade an enormous amount of research has been conducted on serotonin, and more than one thousand articles have been published during these years.[37] As with all substances naturally present in our body, the metabolite serotonin is useful and essential for the activity of our circulatory system, our brain, and digestion.

The most striking fact is that serotonin and LSD are antagonists. This means that if someone takes LSD, the normal func-

[35]Henning Andersen, "The Influence of Hormones on Human Development" in *Human Development,* Frank Falkner, ed., Philadelphia and London: W. B. Saunders Co., 1966, pp. 184–221. See also R. H. Williams, *Textbook on Endocrinology,* Philadelphia and London: W. B. Saunders Co.,

[36]Chemically called 5-hydroxytryptamine.

[37]Boris Sokoloff, *Carcinoid and Serotonin.* New York and Heidelberg: Springer-Verlag, 1968. In this book all the recent discoveries in the field of serotonin are discussed.

tioning of serotonin in the body is disturbed. Serotonin is found in brain tissue and is necessary for the proper activity of our mental functions. When serotonin is increased or decreased in our brain, our mental processes are dangerously affected. When the brain is deficient in serotonin, the ability of learning is sharply decreased. Woolley[38] of the Rockefeller Institute stated that mental deficiency in children is caused by a defect in brain serotonin. This indicates the possibility that the intelligence of children or young men can be affected greatly by derangement in brain serotonin. And J. E. Thuillier[39] expressed the opinion that in all probability a disturbance in brain serotonin leads to psychosis.

Let us now try to understand what occurs when a young man or girl takes LSD. As we said, LSD is an antagonist of serotonin. This means that it can completely eliminate serotonin in the brain. The results are clear. Not only can the intelligence of the boy or girl drop rapidly, but it could cause irreparable damage to the brain structure, making near moron or mentally disturbed individuals out of bright and intelligent ones. Thus we have a tragic picture of youth taking LSD and other similar chemical drugs. They can be transformed into nervous wrecks, of low intelligence and possibly psychotic. And this is what we are witnessing now in this country on a large scale.

There is a revolution in our concept of the old behaviorism —a revolution which will affect all the theories of sociologists, social workers, and psychologists who, in fact, are not apparently cognizant of the tremendous progress and achievement in our knowledge of man as a biological entity. For three decades

[38]D. W. Woolley and T. vanderHoeven, "Alteration in Learning Ability Caused by Changes in Cerebral Serotonin," *Science,* *139*:610, 1963.
[39]J. E. Thuillier, "Psychosis and Autonomic Drugs," in *Chemical Concepts of Psychosis,* ed., New York: McDowell-Obolensky, 1958, pp. 91–101.

the American public has been hypnotized or brainwashed by the assumption, based on Freudian theories, that everything in man's life depends on exterior environmental conditions; that it is society which is responsible for man's failures, his inefficiency, his crime, even his poverty. The scientific discoveries of a psychophysiological nature show, however, that it is not the external environment which makes man what he is but the internal environment. This means that the factors working inside man's body, particularly in the brain—factors of a chemical nature—are actually the major forces which form his personality and affect his behavior-forces, many of which are of a hereditary nature. *The emphasis on external environmental forces which are supposed to affect man's behavior is changing to the new concept, that of the internal environment.* Up to now, in spite of all the fantastic progress in biological sciences, which has brought mankind the armaments to fight infectious and chronic diseases, to transplant organs, to travel to the moon, to prolong the life span of man for almost 10 years, the biological sciences were and still are ignored by sociologists, psychologists, and social workers. Man as a living individual entity is ignored by them. They have been building a society as if individuals were insignificant pawns in their speculative planning. They accepted Freudian postulates, which like their own, were erected on sand, without scientific background. The new concept of man as a biological integral entity is destroying Freud's "house of cards." The time has arrived when our sociologists, psychologists, and the politicians dominating our sociopolitical system should learn a little more about what a human individual actually is.

PART TWO

•

Our Permissive Society

•

6

.

Crime in America

• •

An Introductory Note

For more than three decades, American intellectuals, the flower of our society, have been subjected to the influences of Freudian doctrine and ethics. As was said, and we hope was proved, the basis of the Freudian movement is extreme permissiveness, directed first of all against Society or The Establishment. Without exaggeration, one must acknowledge the phenomenal success of Freudian permissiveness in all aspects of American life: crime, narcotics, family, education and campus riots, sex, and even in the Supreme Court decisions. Many intellectuals call the present permissiveness drive a revolution, one which, according to them, would open new horizons and a new era for the American people.

In the second part of this book I present the factual picture of what is going on in our country as a result of extreme permissiveness. I present the events as reported in newspapers and journals, with little or no comment. I offer the reader the opportunity to draw his own conclusions about what might be called the "Freudian Revolution."

"The root cause of most crime is poverty," declared John Lindsay, Mayor of New York City.[1] "Poverty is the cause of violent crime," concluded the President's Commission on the cause and prevention of violence.

"Almost 4.5 million serious crimes were recorded during 1968. Crime was up 122 percent, and the crime rate up 99 percent, as compared with 1960 . . . a 17 percent rise over 1967. Daytime burglaries of residences rose 247 percent from 1960 to 1968. Property valued at more than $1.7 billion was stolen as a result of 261,730 robberies, 1,825,000 larcenies, 3,442,800 burglaries, and 777,800 auto thefts."[2]

Most striking is a violent crime which cannot be related to poverty in any way: *forcible rape.*

According to the FBI report[3] there were 22,970 cases of forcible rape in 1965; 25,330 in 1966; 27,100 in 1967, and 31,060 reported rape cases in 1968. This vicious crime has increased by 84 percent since 1960. These figures are underestimated and it is calculated that the actual number of forcible rapes is double that registered by the police, and that the total figures of rape for 1968 are close to 60,000. As the FBI states: "Law enforcement administrators recognize that this offense [rape of women] is probably the most under-reported crime by

[1] The Miami Beach Conference, July 31, 1968.
[2] *Crime in the United States,* FBI, 1968, p. 1.
[3] *Ibid.,* pp. 11–13.

victims to police due primarily to fear and/or embarrassment on the part of many victims."[4]

This crime occurs most often in cities with 250,000 or more inhabitants. In 1968, this group of cities registered an upward trend of 15 percent, while the volume increased by 6 percent in the suburban areas.

Generally speaking, according to reported assaults, there is a woman raped every 15 minutes in this country. By adding the estimated number of rapes not reported to the police, one may say that every 8 to 10 minutes a woman is raped.

In New York City, 2,781 women were raped in 1968, or about seven women every day (not counting the unreported rapes). In small cities this crime is much less in evidence. As an example, in Green Bay, Wisconsin there were only five cases of forcible rape in 1968, or 3.5 cases per 100,000. In Springfield–Holyoke, Massachusetts no case of forcible rape was reported in 1968.

The FBI stresses the fact that males 17- to 20-year age group constituted the greatest concentration of arrests for forcible rape in 1968.

Forcible rape is not a topic of discussion by politicians and intellectuals. In his political discourses Mayor Lindsay never mentioned that seven reported forcible rapes, and perhaps an equal number of unreported cases occur in his city every day. The newspapers and magazines also avoid reporting the cases of forcible rape, although a whole book could be filled with the tragic stories of unfortunate women forced to submit to this humiliating assault. Only a few cases are found in the newspapers.

Forcible rape occurs in the United States not, for the most part, in isolated areas but in the central part of a city. For

[4] *Ibid.*, p. 13.

example, the Associated Press reported that in Kansas City a Catholic nun was sexually assaulted and a priest was beaten, shot, and robbed near Kansas City's south central business district early in the morning. The unidentified nun and the priest, identified as Father Charles Tobin of St. James Catholic Church, said they were approached by two armed men while talking in their parked car.

This occurred near the Country Club Plaza, where they had driven after a church function at Bishop Hogan High School Friday night.

The men forced them to drive to 44th Street where the priest was told to get out of the car, and then beaten, shot in a leg, robbed, and left behind.

The nun said the men then drove her somewhere in the vicinity of 33rd Street where she was criminally assaulted twice, and beaten. The two men then fled.

In New York City, the tragic stories of rape are so frequent that only occasionally are the offenders caught. Such was the case of three women living on the east side in a residential part of the city. The story recounts that a truck driver was held in $25,000 bail on charges of raping three young women.

The police identified the suspect as Carmine Villano, 28 years old, of 185 Skillman Avenue, Brooklyn, who was booked at the East 67th Street station on charges of rape, sodomy, and assault.

According to the police, the three women, 25, 27, and 28 years old were watching television in their apartment in the 80's at 10 P.M. on a Friday when Villano allegedly entered through a partly open door.

The police said that he forced the women to submit by holding a knife at their throats, each time warning the other two that a scream for help would mean the death of the one he was attacking.

However, one of the women managed to slip into the living room where she quietly dialed the police emergency telephone number, 911, and whispered, "There's three girls being held by a madman with a knife."

The call was relayed to a patrol car at 81st Street and York Avenue, manned by a sergeant and two patrolmen of the Youth Division. When they burst into the apartment, Villano allegedly lunged with the knife at the young woman who had made the phone call. Patrolman Robert Bienemann grabbed the suspect.

There seems to be a definite trend toward what might be called "mass rape" or "gang rape." A group of young men attack a lone woman, or sometimes two or more, often in daylight in the center of a city, taking the victim to an isolated place where they engage in a sexual orgy, raping the woman again and again.

The UPI reported that on Thanksgiving Day in Chicago, two nurses were raped several times by two armed men on a lonely west side elevated platform while they were waiting for the subway train.

Florida newspapers reported[5] that four Negroes, armed with broken bottles, a board, and possibly a pistol, raped two white girls on a Thursday evening while the girl's dates were forced to stand aside.

The two white couples were parked behind Tigertown near Lake Parker late Thursday night when the assailants came at them out of the night and surrounded the automobile.

The girls, both from Haines City, were taken out of the car and raped repeatedly by the Negroes. The girls were 15 and 18 years old.

According to one of the white boys, he and his date had been

[5]Quoted from the article by Frank Roderus, Lakeland (Florida) *Ledger* staff writer.

sitting in the back seat of the car when the Negro men, all described as being between 20 and 25 years of age, appeared on both sides of the auto.

One of the assailants opened the driver's door, jerked the keys from the ignition switch, and claimed that he had a pistol. The boys were slapped and threatened, and all four of the occupants of the car were told that their throats would be cut if they did not cooperate.

The Negroes took the girls away separately, raped them, then returned them to the car.

With one of the Negroes driving, both couples were taken to Simpson Park swimming pool where one of the girls was raped again.

Finally, the Negroes told the couples to get back in the car, leave and "forget this ever happened."

The UPI tells a horror story that occurred with high school students in Jacksonville, Florida, on March 14, 1970.

A venture to a "haunted house" turned into a night of terror for a group of high school students who were herded into a bathroom by two armed Negroes while two of the girls were carried off and raped, police said.

Police said a group of 11 students from Jacksonville's Ribault High, including eight girls, had gone to an old vacant house near the downtown section of the city about 11 P.M. on a Friday night. Two young Negroes barged in, one armed with a sawed-off shotgun and the other with a knife, and demanded to know if the white youths had any "reefers."

When they were told no, police said, the two Negroes passed around a hat and forced the whites to put their money in it. They picked out two of the girls—one 17 and the other 18—to leave with them and threatened to knife anyone who tried to follow them.

"That's the easiest way to kill someone," one of the intruders was quoted as saying.

Police said the girls were taken to another vacant house where the two Negroes were joined by three others. The men yanked the girls' sweaters and blouses over their heads and sexually assaulted the older girl four times and the other twice.

Later the girls were driven a short distance away and released and the car was taken back to the "haunted" house.

Washington newspapers gave considerable publicity to a similar case of a "mass rape." Mrs. X., the wife of a State Department official was walking her two small poodles a few blocks from her home. It was a sunny morning and nothing indicated the forthcoming tragedy. Not far from Pennsylvania Avenue she turned to a side street where there was a house with a large garden, surrounded by a high wall. The house was closed because the owners were on a European trip. Suddenly Mrs. X. was seized by four young Negroes. One, the youngest boy, took charge of her dogs, while the other three dragged Mrs. X. into the garden. For two hours she was raped repeatedly by the assailants, while the fourth young man was on watch. At last she was left alone. She went to the nearest police station where she was met, as she complained later, with coldness, if not hostility. "Nothing can be done," she was informed. "It's a common case."

Nothing is heard in the newspapers about the suffering, pain and humiliation the raped woman goes through. No one has raised a voice against the shame of this crime, neither U. S. Senators or Congressmen, nor newspaper commentators. Yet often, more frequently than one assumes, the life and spirit of a raped woman are gravely affected.

One case took place in the center of New York, on the east

side. It was late in the afternoon and the street was quite busy with passersby going home from their offices. A young married woman, a librarian in charge of a bookstore, remained in the store after the other employees had left. She was ready to leave the store when three men entered, locked the door, seized her, and dragged her into the back room where the book stocks were kept. For three hours they raped her repeatedly. They were brutal, she commented later. This woman had a complete breakdown, her family life was ruined and for several months after the assault she was unable to regain her mental and physical health.

According to the FBI:[6] "In 1968, approximately 47 percent of the persons arrested for forcible rape were Negroes, 51 percent whites, and all other races comprised the remainder."

There are some indications that forcible rape is taking on an ever more violent and brutal aspect. In a number of reported cases, the women were killed after being raped.

All in all, according to the FBI, *during the five-year period 1965–69, there were 139,700 reported cases of forcible rape of women. If we accept the statement of the FBI that this crime is the most under-reported, in all probability the total number of forcible rape cases during this period would be close to 200,000.*

The basis of this violent crime is the extreme permissiveness in our country and the weakness of law enforcement. The following story which was brought to the author's attention fully illustrates that permissiveness affects not only criminals but even law-abiding citizens.

A large new settlement in lower Westchester County is inhabited by a white middle-class population, with houses in the

[6]*Crime in the United States,* FBI, 1968.

$20,000 range, a movie theater, a bowling alley, several churches, three drug stores. The majority of homeowners are relatively young, and are employed in nearby White Plains and other towns. Five families living in this community became friends. The five husbands first met at the bowling alley. Two were accountants, one a supermarket assistant manager, one a commercial artist, and one a salesman for a chemical company. Soon their wives met and now and then gave modest parties for the group at their homes. Three men and two women were college graduates. All of them were in their late twenties or early thirties, the women rather attractive, and most of them were childless. Only one of the families had a son, and he was at boarding school. The men worked hard, the women remaining at home, typical housewives. One evening the five men were in the local bar to which they always adjourned after bowling. While sitting there, the artist, Jack N., remarked that he noticed that his wife of five years seemed to be bored. "There is no fire in our married life." The others agreed and admitted that a similar situation also existed in their lives. What could be done to make their marriages more passionate?

"Look at the hippies," Paul, the accountant, remarked. "They have all they want."

"I have a plan," Jack said. "A justifiable rape." And he explained to the others what he meant. "One evening, I'll leave home telling Louise that I'll be away for two or three hours. I'll give you the key to our house. You four go there and rape my wife."

"What a horrible idea!" exclaimed Peter, the supermarket assistant manager. "But your wife will fight. It's dangerous."

"Not at all," Jack retorted. "Use force, if needed. At the end she'll be pleased, since she knows all of you."

"And after? . . ." Paul asked.

"Next will be your wife, and so on."

The friends discussed this plan, at first hesitantly and reluctantly, but gradually they became quite enthusiastic. Three days later, the plan was put into action. When four of them entered Jack's house, Louise, in a transparent robe, was watching TV, with a highball in her hand. She was astonished by their visit. Yet she suspected nothing. They approached her. One of the men took her by the arm. "What do you want?" she cried. "You'll see." They seized her, not brutally, and undressed her. She fought like a wildcat. Two men held her firmly. One after the other they raped her. She calmed down. They repeated the attack. There was no fight left in her. Following Jack's advice, they were very kind to her. They dressed her and offered her a drink. She took it and smiled slightly. "I'll tell Jack. He'll kill all of you." But there was no anger in her voice. They left after kissing her. Thirty minutes later Jack arrived. He found his wife watching TV with a highball in her hand. She yawned.

"How are you?" he asked.

"Sleepy" was her answer.

A few days later they visited Paul's home. It all went as smoothly with Marie as it had with Louise.

The next week, when they went to Peter's home, the reaction of Dora, his wife, was more violent. She fought, she cried, she was hysterical, but at the end she resigned herself as the other women had done.

When the circle was ended and all five wives had received the same treatment, the husbands started another tour. This time they received a much warmer welcome from the wives. All except Dora, who was angry to see the offenders entering her home again. She tried to reach the telephone but was prevented by Jack. The other four wives seemed to enjoy the visit of their husband's friends. They accepted the invasion with laughter and more response.

This went on for several months. Soon the wives learned that each of them was treated in the same fashion. Yet this knowledge only lessened the tension which had been present before they learned the truth. Even Dora now reacted as the other wives did. Now and then they had home parties with all the husbands and wives present. When there was no more secrecy about it, they all became even more friendly with each other. "A true family of ten," Louise remarked. Soon, however, the police were informed about the peculiar gatherings in their homes. But there was no available evidence for prosecution and they were left alone. A little later Jack and Peter moved to another town, and this pseudo-criminal rape activity was ended.

This story, possibly one of many similar cases going on in this country, emphasizes the deep demoralization of our middle class, or rather of a small part of it. Here again, even more obviously than in any other case, no relationship can be established between poverty and forcible rape, and only extreme permissiveness can be blamed for such behavior.

Car Theft

"In 1968, 777,800 motor vehicles were reported stolen compared to 654,900 thefts in 1967. Automobile thefts occurred at an average of more than one a minute throughout the year. . . . As was experienced in 1967, seasonal variations during 1968 disclosed auto theft reached its peak in the fall of the year with October recording the high month in volume. . . . This crime has been steadily rising each year since 1960 with an overall increase of 139 percent over the nine-year period. . . . Auto theft rates clearly indicate that this crime is primarily a big city problem. Although police were able to recover 86 percent of the stolen vehicles, the remaining unrecovered 14 percent repre-

sented a dollar loss in excess of $100 million to the victims."[7]
Only 19 percent of these thefts were solved by arrest of the
offender. "In 1968, 61 percent of all persons arrested for this
crime were under 18 years and 16 percent were under 15 years
of age."[8] Only 5 percent of persons arrested in 1968 were
females. Yet female arrests for auto theft increased by 26 percent. "Whites made up 62 percent of the arrests for auto theft,
Negroes 35 percent, and all other races the remaining 3 percent.
*The most impressive fact is that 80 percent of persons arrested
for auto thefts were repeaters."* This means that during the
five-year period, 1963–68, the great majority of offenders repeated their criminal act. Auto theft does not solve the economic problem of this type of offender since in the majority of
cases the autos were recovered within 48 hours. Thus it was an
act of hooliganism or permissiveness. In the case of 14 percent
of thefts in which the autos were not recovered there was apparently a criminal organization which managed to dispose of the
stolen automobiles. Therefore one may ask: *"Is poverty the
cause of auto theft?"*

Murder

"In 1968, there were estimated to be 13,650 murders committed in the United States. This represents a numerical increase
of 1,560 homicides when compared to 12,090 murders recorded
in 1967."[10] There was a trend toward a decrease of murder cases
during the years 1960–1963, which was followed by a steady
growth in homicides during 1964–68. Males outnumbered
females as victims of murder three to one in 1968. As in the
prior year 45 of every 100 victims were white, and 54 were

[7] *Crime in the United States,* FBI, 1968, p. 26.
[8] *Ibid.,* p. 26.
[9] *Ibid.,* p. 38.
[10] *Ibid.,* p. 6.

Negroes. "The significant fact emerges that most murders are committed by relatives of the victim or persons acquainted with the victim. . . . In 1968 killing within the family made up over one-fourth of all murders. . . . In situations involving husband and wife, the wife was victim in 54 percent of the cases and the husband in 46 percent. In these incidents, 48 percent of the victims were white, 51 percent were Negroes."[11] Since Negroes constitute only 11 percent of the total population, the frequency of killing wife or husband is about five times greater among Negroes than whites.

The Lakeland (Florida) *Ledger* illustrates a typical family murder.

A Christmas eve family argument ended in the shooting death of a Lakeland man. His 18-year-old son Paul was jailed on a charge of murder.

About 7:15 P.M. on a Wednesday, Joseph H. Kirk, 65, was shot in the side with a .30-.30 rifle which was believed to be a Christmas present to his son from his wife, Marie.

Sheriff Monroe Brannen said the shooting was apparently the result of a long family argument which erupted into violence.

Kirk died on the operating table at Lakeland General hospital at 11:50 P.M.

Paul Kirk was released from the Polk County jail under $5,000 bond Thursday and continued attending school.

The UPI reported a case in Gaines, Pennsylvania—a 15-year-old boy was charged with murder in the shotgun death of a girl hunting companion a few miles from this rural nothern Pennsylvania community.

Trooper William Herbst said the body of Charlette Good-

[11] *Ibid.*, p. 8.

wyn, also 15, was found Wednesday, shoved beneath the ice on a creek. She had been shot three times with a 12-gauge shotgun.

Jack Lee Thompson was arrested at his home hours later, Herbst said.

Two other companions, Dennis Ellis and Viola Hoppe, both 15, witnessed the shooting, then fled.

"We can't make any sense out of it," Herbst remarked.

It appears that the four young people were friends until the moment of the shooting. They all attended the same school and lived in Gaines.

Also included are murders which were not solved and the motivation not detected.

In Detroit, the UPI reported that a Negro doctor, who had brought life to thousands, left it, sprawled on a sidewalk in the black neighborhood he loved and served.

Police called the killing of 49-year old Dr. Arthur Drayton Harris "wanton and senseless." That did not lessen the shock for Detroit's medical community. Nor did the fact that two 15-year-old Negro youths were being held for his murder ease the fears of Detroit's other black doctors.

"There is this continual feeling of fear," said Dr. Leon Dickinson. "And now Dr. Harris . . . nobody had anything but love for him and now he's shot down for no reason at all. Why does it happen?"

A terrifying mass murder in Mesa, Arizona was reported by the AP.

An 18-year-old high school senior forced seven women and girls to lie face down on the floor of a beauty school, and he killed five of them.

Police Sgt. Ray Gomez said Robert Smith of Mesa admitted

the shooting and told him he first got the idea after reading of mass killings elsewhere.

The victims were Mrs. Joyce Sellers, 27, and her 3½-year-old daughter, Debra; Mary Margaret Olsen, and Glenda Carter, all of Mesa; and Carol Farmer, Williams Air Force Base.

Mrs. Sellers' three-month-old daughter, Tamma Lynn, was critically wounded. An employee of the school, Bonita Sue Harris, was wounded less seriously.

The gunman forced the women to lie in a circle, like spokes of a wheel, and calmly walked around the outside, shooting each in the back of the head.

Smith was arrested at the scene.

On August 1, Charles Joseph Whitman, 25, killed 15 people in Austin, Texas, before a policeman shot him dead on the 27th floor observation deck of a tower at the University of Texas.

Whitman had killed his wife and mother before ascending the tower, where he killed 13 and wounded 31 with three rifles, a shotgun, and two pistols. One of the wounded died later.

On July 14, eight student nurses were murdered in their house on the south side of Chicago. They had been strangled, stabbed, or had their throats cut.

Another mass murder was reported from Cincinnati by the AP.

The methodical police search for clues in the grisly slaying of a young family of three continued with little progress reported.

The bodies of the parents and their four-year-old daughter, stabbed repeatedly, were found Tuesday night in their suburban Bridgetown, Ohio home. Police theorized they were murdered late Sunday.

Frank Murray of the Washington AP reported that three pretty blondes were savagely stabbed to death in a Washington, D.C., suburb within 16 days, and some authorities fear they face a butcher on the Beltway.

Other officers said the murders were yet to be firmly linked. But the army of young career women from across the nation— many of them living in apartment complexes dotting the super-highway that girdles the capital like a belt—cared little whether the killer is one or several. Fright was their roommate.

"Since the killings I don't even go out in the hall by myself," said one Capitol Hill worker.

Dead were Sherry Bristol Kennedy, 14, a junior high school Spanish language whiz, dumped in a snowy ravine with an icepick in her skull; Catherine O'Brien Kalberer, 33, a Shakespeare scholar and high school English teacher, whose body was waffled with 124 slashes; and Donna Sue Oglesby, 18, an FBI file clerk, stripped naked and stabbed with scissors.

Many cases of murder remain unsolved, such as the case of two girls in Tallahassee, Florida. The beaten and stabbed bodies of two popular high school girls were found sprawled on a bed of pine needles in a wooded recreation area.

These murders occurred almost a year after the slayings of state department of education official Robert W. Sims, 42, and his wife and 12-year-old daughter. No suspects were reported in either case. There was no indication of a connection between the Sims murders, still unsolved, and the deaths of the two girls.

The great majority of murder cases have no motivation of robbery. It is estimated that only seven to eight percent of all homicides were the result of attempted or consummated robbery.

One case of robbery-murder involved a socialite killed in

Morristown, New Jersey. According to the UPI, Mrs. Dorothy Beck Palmer, 57-year-old wife of industrial expert H. Bruce Palmer, battled a knife-wielding intruder for her life with a can of paralyzing chemical spray, and lost.

Police said the tall dark-haired assailant killed the attractive greying matron with one stab wound in the heart in spite of her efforts to immobilize him with a can of mace spray she kept by her bedside.

The intruder entered the house by breaking a window in a guest room, apparently with robbery as a motive.

A good description of the murderer was given police by the family maid who discovered him near Mrs. Palmer's body and fled the house for help.

Apparently there is no evidence that homicides are caused by poverty. Homicides are committed either for personal or emotional reasons, or by maniacs. And in most murder cases, the permissiveness syndrome, overpoweringly dominant, and the absence of self-control, are major contributing factors.[12]

Assaults

"Most aggravated assaults occur within the family unit or among neighbors or acquaintances. The victim and offender relationship, as well as the very nature of the attack makes this crime similar to murder. . . . In the calendar year 1968 there was an estimated total of 282,400 aggravated assaults. This is an increase of 29,100 offenses over the previous year . . . and 86 percent over 1960. . . . A comparison for 1968 with the year 1960 reflects that arrests of young persons under 18 increased 118 percent while those for adults were up 39 percent.[13]

---

[12]Philip G. Roche, *The Criminal Mind,* New York: Farrar, Straus and Cudahy, 1958.
[13]*Crime in the United States,* FBI, pp. 9–11.

This category of crime revealed two essential facts: (a) the tendency of Americans to lose their self-control, associated with pronounced permissiveness syndrome; and (b) that the generation under 18 years of age demonstrated three times greater increase in commission of assaults than the older population. The permissive conduct of youth reflects the degree of demoralization of their personality, and the immaturity in their behavior. In the category of assaults *there is no evidence or indication that poverty plays a significant, if any, role.* In middle-class or in low-income groups of the population, aggravated assault is equally frequent.

Robbery

"During the calendar year 1968, there were an estimated 261,730 robberies committed in the United States. This represents a significant increase over 202,050 robberies which occurred in 1967; a 30 percent rise over 1967, and since 1960 this violent crime has increased 144 percent in the United States. Among the types of robberies there has been a sharp increase of 302 percent in bank robbery since 1960. During the same period gas or service station hold-ups have risen 187 percent, chain store robberies 210 percent, robberies in residences nearly doubled and hold-ups of other commercial or business establishments rose 107 percent."[14] In 1968 law enforcement agencies were successful in solving only 27 percent of these crimes, *a decrease of 8 percent when compared with 1967.* "Arrest data discloses that 75 percent of the persons arrested were under 25 years of age, 56 percent under 21 years, and 33 percent of the persons arrested were under 18. From the standpoint of race, 62 percent of those arrested were Negroes, 36 percent were white, and all other races made up the remaining 2 percent."[15] Of persons arrested for robberies 60 percent were repeaters or,

[14] *Crime in the United States,* FBI, 1968, p. 13.
[15] *Ibid.,* p. 17.

one may say, professional criminals. The number of persons taking part in robberies is not available in the FBI reports, but one assumes that in most cases, an average of two persons were involved in the act of robbery. Since 261,730 cases occurred in 1968, probably about 500,000 criminals were involved in this crime during one calendar year. The FBI estimated that about $70 million were taken from the victims, bodily injuries not included. Thus each criminal earned an average of only $140.00 from his crime. This seems to confirm the cliché that crime does not pay. The majority of the offenders were young men. *One wonders, in view of 60 percent of repeaters in this group, if the extreme permissiveness in our society is not a factor in their crime, rather than poverty.*

A story told by an AP reporter makes clear how deficient is police protection against robbery.

Frank Wingate, of Pensacola, Florida, a Navy veteran saw more action in a recent week than in three years of military service. He had more than his share of the robberies that had plagued Florida neighborhood shops and liquor stores.

For the fourth time in a week, the 63-year-old liquor store clerk found himself staring down the cold barrel of a revolver.

The robber was the seventeenth Wingate had faced since he started working at the Club Garden liquor store seven years before. And he readily admitted that "it's become somewhat nerve-racking."

"It was bad enough to have it happen just every now and then," Wingate said later, "but four times in one week is about all I can stand."

There's just "no getting used to facing up to a bandit's gun no matter how many times it happens," said the slender, mild-spoken clerk.

"Frankly, it scares the wits out of me every time," he admitted.

"Some people have asked me why I don't yell or run or something. But let me tell you, when you're standing there with a gun barrel pointed directly at you by a man who is as apt to shoot you as not, it's a horse of a different color."

In spite of the robberies, Wingate had no intention of quitting or changing his job.

On the basis of the FBI figures there are at large in the streets of the United States, particularly in large cities, about 400,000 to 500,000 criminals who specialize in armed robbery. More than half are repeaters, hopelessly involved in crime. Can one state that poverty is the cause of robbery? Are the bank robbers poverty-stricken men? Or are we dealing with professional criminals? No wonder Philip Wechsler, Lakeland *Ledger* staff writer, writes from New York that "the fear of crime in the streets, particularly in major cities, has prompted more and more women to refuse night shifts or overtime work during evening hours.

"As a result companies are spending millions of dollars, in addition to higher night pay, on safety precautions to attract women to evening work."

Burglary

Burglary is the commonest crime in this country. "An estimated total of 1,828,000 burglaries occurred during 1968. There was an increase of 223,200 offenses over 1967. Since 1960 burglary has increased 104 percent. . . . Burglary is a crime of stealth and opportunity committed by amateurs and professionals alike. . . . In 1968 property owners suffered an economic loss of $545 million, with an average dollar loss of $298.00 per burglary."[16] "Arrests of individuals under the age of 15 increased 70 percent and those under the age of 18, almost 70

---

[16]*Crime in the United States,* FBI, p. 17.

percent. . . . Of the total, young persons under 18 accounted for 55 percent of all arrests for this crime . . . *Arrests of whites outnumbered Negroes by almost two to one.* [17]

From these figures it appears that the majority of offenders in this category of crime were under 18. And that Negroes were in a considerable minority as compared with whites. Since it often is said that Negroes chiefly are affected by poverty, something is wrong with linking poverty with burglary. From various reports it was found that the young offenders are from middle-class groups. If this is true, burglary, so enormously increased, reflects the absence of self-control, the unlimited permissiveness of family and environment. With the repeaters for this crime constituting 60 percent we have in this country almost one million burglars.

The AP reported that six young men were charged in 40 burglaries in a lower Westchester County, New York. Police said these youths were members of a teenage burglary band linked to 40 crimes involving businesses in the Westchester–Putnam area. Four of them were under 16 years old.

Lawrence Byrnes, 17, of Yorktown, and Frank Pace, 16 also of Yorktown, were booked on several counts of burglary, grand larceny, petty larceny, and criminal mischief. They were released in the custody of their parents pending probable grand jury action.

Four others, described as area youths, were also charged but names have been withheld because of their ages. These cases will be handled by the Westchester Family Court. The boys belonged to families not affected by poverty. In his report from Washington, the late Drew Pearson, discussing the burglaries which occurred during the riots following the assassination of Dr. King, stressed the fact "that some of the most determined looters [burglars] in Washington were government

---

[17] *Ibid.,* p. 18.

employees. District of Columbia judges, who sat all night
processing the 4,000 arrested looters, were flabbergasted at
the fact that a predominant number worked for the government." They did not belong to the poverty-stricken population groups.

Shoplifting offers an interesting psychological concept of a
modern criminal mind. Are the poverty-stricken persons of our
country to be blamed for this type of larceny? Hundreds of
stories have been told about well-to-do women caught shoplifting. Apparently shoplifting, which has increased by 134 percent
since 1960, also is becoming fashionable with radical youth
from wealthy families. Carll Tucker, columnist for a Westchester county newspaper[18] reported his conversation with a friend,
a self-justifying "revolutionary" shoplifter.

> Recently, I was lunching with a radical friend, and the subject
> of shoplifting came up.
> "Oh, I shoplift all the time," he said.
> "Why?" I asked.
> "For the hell of it."
> "I think it's remarkable that someone with ideals as exalted
> as yours should approve of petty thievery."
> "No. All I'm doing is stealing from the system. It's not like
> snatching pocketbooks."
> "But you don't really believe it's the store that pays for their
> losses. It's the consumer who eventually bears the burden in
> higher prices. And certainly you're not opposed to the con-
> sumer?"
> "All consumers can steal if they want to. That'd really screw
> up the works."
> "But you know that won't happen. And meanwhile you, who
> can afford to buy the goods, steal them, while those who can ill
> afford it are forced to pay higher prices. In other words, the
> working man, with whom you claim to be allied, is paying for
> your symbolic protest against the system."

[18]Carll Tucker, III, "Speaking of Shoplifting," *Patent Trader,* Mount Kisco, New
York, March 21, 1970.

"They're free to steal, if they want."

"But they can't afford to get caught, like you can."

"Your hang-up, man, is that you accept this whole bag. You accept the validity of this system. You think it's right that one class of people should have all the money and impose their will upon the rest. You think it's right that the workingman is paid only a fraction of his output. You think it's right that this store should take huge profits out of the backs of consumers. Well, I don't agree. So I don't pay their huge profits. I don't pay them anything. And if nobody paid, there wouldn't be any store. And if there wasn't any store there wouldn't be any capitalists. And if there weren't any capitalists, there wouldn't be any more oppression. You see, I think it's all wrong. I think we should start again. And shoplifting is just one little way to fight the system."

Here is an amazing case of extraordinary permissiveness, colored and justified by supposedly "revolutionary idealism." The fact is that the "radical" shoplifter did not give the stolen goods to poor men, but used them himself. This is one of many cases of shoplifting by "idealistic" youth.

Shoplifting has become epidemic in this country. According to the recent FBI report, shoplifting nationally has increased more than 150 percent since 1969. And it is not getting any better. The value of stolen goods runs into billions of dollars. What is the basis of this extraordinary phenomenon? According to Dr. Joseph Price, of the Winter Haven (Florida) Community Mental Center: "Many people feel that there is no harm in shoplifting. . . . I think most people shoplift for the thrill of it, just to see if they can get away with it." But the actual basis of this fast-growing shoplifting epidemic is the disrespect for law and appalling permissiveness in this country. Certainly poverty is not the cause of shoplifting.

There is one important question about crime in America, a question which is avoided by newspapers and writers: the steady increase of crime by Negroes.

In their recent article published in the liberal *Newsweek* (March 8, 1971), Peter Goldman and Don Holt wrote:

> Street crime has contributed powerfully to the malaise of the nation's decaying big cities and street crime in urban America has become in large and growing measure Negro crime. The subject has until lately been thought too painful for public discussion; to raise it has been considered treasonable among blacks and racist among sympathetic whites. But the statistics command attention. One little-noted staff study for Lyndon Johnson's commission on violence showed urban arrest rates 10 to 18 times higher for Negroes than for whites in serious crimes of violence and up to 20 times higher for black teenagers. Another, a 17-city survey, found blacks suspected of 72 percent of the criminal homicides, 74 percent of the aggravated assaults, 70 percent of the rapes and 85 percent of the robberies in which the police made the arrest.

Such are the figures of impartial statistical surveys. As expected, the authors try to explain and justify the enormity of crimes, including forcible rapes of women, by the poverty among blacks. Yet the evidence fully indicates that the permissive syndrome dominates the large part of black America. Not only it is unrestricted and uncontrolled but it is growing steadily.

Why has there been such an enormous and steady increase in crime in this country during the last five to six years? J. Edgar Hoover, Director of the Federal Bureau of Investigation, is trying to give an answer. Mildly and diplomatically, he recounted the following story:

> The story is told of a mythical young knight who rode out to encounter his first fire-breathing dragon. When he spotted the beast, he froze with fear. He closed his eyes and hoped that the monster would go away. He was wrong, of course, and the dragon devoured him.

We have on the loose in our country today a predatory monster called crime. It is growing in size and violence. Its far-reaching forages threaten every city and hamlet in the Nation, and it strikes fear in the hearts and minds of the law-abiding public. It is ripping away the very fiber of our society and our system of government.

. . . The story of alarming crime increases each year is not a new story. It is old and it is true. One appalling aspect is the fact that many people in positions of responsibility continue to deny this truth. They prefer to close their eyes and hope that crime, if ignored, will go away. Here, as with the mythical young knight, this wistful approach is doomed to failure.

Concerted efforts have been made to minimize the seriousness of the crime problem and to explain away the shocking truths behind crime statistics.

. . . The answer to our Nation's crime problem will be found in direct, positive action—not by waiting and hoping the problem will go away. A good beginning would be to let the guilty criminal know that when he is arrested, he will be promptly prosecuted and substantially punished for his misdeeds. A good time to begin would be NOW.

Why is crime in this country snowballing so fast? Technically speaking, one of the problems is the lack of police manpower. A survey of 36 police departments showed that not one is up to authorized strength. Numerous police officers have been killed in the line of duty. Thus in ". . . 1968 the trend established in prior years continued in that more law enforcement officers met death by criminal action when attempting to arrest than from any other cause."[19] Sixty-five police officers were killed in 1968, and 475 during 1960–1968. The figures for 1970 are expected to be much higher.

Yet the U.S. spent $7.3 billion in 1969 to combat crime, or $36.50 for every American. Compiled by the Census Bureau and the Law Enforcement Assistance Administration, the report, released December 23, 1970, marks the first such nationwide survey of how much money and how many people are

[19]*Crime in the United States,* FBI, 1968, pp. 46–7.

involved in U.S. law enforcement and prevention.

There were some 730,000 persons—70 percent of them in local governments—working in various phases of law enforcement including police, judges, prosecuting agencies, defense of the poor, prisons, and jails.

Some $4.4 billion was spent nationwide to maintain police forces, compared to about $1.5 billion in correctional institutions.

Another $1 billion went for the judiciary, $369 million for prosecution, and nearly $78 million to pay for court-appointed lawyers.

The breakdown indicates 64 percent of the $7.3 billion was spent by local governments, 25 percent at the state level, and 11 percent by the federal government.

The country's 43 largest cities spent 10.4 percent of their budget fighting crime, the report said.

In spite of this large expenditure on the fight against crime, the situation is far from being under control. On the contrary, crime is growing fast, reaching incredible proportions.

There is only one answer to this puzzle. There is only one logical explanation of this phenomenon. There is an atmosphere of extreme permissiveness which favors and invites crime, which rejects law and order in America. For this the liberal intellectuals should be blamed unhesitatingly. For the American liberal intellectuals accepted fully the principles of Freudian doctrine, which is indulgent toward criminals whom it considers victims of society. Almost word for word, liberal intellectuals repeat the Freudian motto: *Man is not responsible for what he is doing against the laws of his country for society;* or, *The Establishment is responsible for his actions.*

A typical representative of the permissive liberal intellectuals is Ramsay Clark, who served as Attorney General under President Lyndon B. Johnson, and who contributed considerably to the promotion of the permissive attitude toward crime. While the official head of the fight against crime, he repeatedly stressed his opposition to the term "law and order," finding excuses in the poverty and other social conditions existing in America. He restated his view on the CBS television program "Face the Nation" on November 22, 1970. He denied that the American people are afraid of criminals. Instead he expressed the belief that President Nixon's call for the fight against crime frightened the American public. "Never in history have so many been so frightened by so few," he said.

J. Edgar Hoover reacted to Clark's statement in an interview with a Washington *Post* reporter:

"There never was a worse Attorney General than Ramsay Clark. You never knew which way he was going to flop on an issue. . . . Clark was [as Attorney General] . . . a jellyfish."

Not only the Department of Justice, headed by Clark, but also the U. S. Supreme Court was—and to some extent still is —contaminated by Freudian ideas of permissiveness in the fight against crime.

Severe criticism of the Supreme Court rulings was expressed by many law enforcement persons. It was said that many rulings of the Supreme Court have made it almost impossible to bring offenders to punishment by the courts due to these interpretations of the criminal procedures.

Here are several decisions of the Supreme Court, which have reversed convictions of offenders in spite of quite convincing evidence of their guilt.

No. 759. Miranda v. Arizona

On March 13, 1963, petitioner, Ernesto Miranda, was arrested at his home and taken in custody to a Phoenix police station. He was there identified by the complaining witness. The police then took him to "Interrogation Room No. 2" of the detective bureau. There he was questioned by two police officers. The officers admitted at trial that Miranda was not advised that he had a right to have an attorney present. Two hours later, the officers emerged from the interrogation room with a written confession signed by Miranda. At the top of the statement was a typed paragraph stating that the confession was made voluntarily, without threats or promises of immunity and "with full knowledge of my legal rights, understanding any statement I make may be used against me."

At his trial before a jury, the written confession was admitted into evidence over the objection of defense counsel, and the officers testified to the prior oral confession made by Miranda during the interrogation. Miranda was found guilty of kidnapping and rape. He was sentenced to 20 to 30 years' imprisonment on each count, the sentences to run concurrently. On appeal, the Supreme Court of Arizona held that Miranda's constitutional rights were not violated in obtaining the confession and affirmed the conviction. 98 Ariz. 18, 401 P. 2d 721. In reaching its decision, the court emphasized heavily the fact that Miranda did not specifically request counsel.

We reverse. From the testimony of the officers and by the admission of respondent, it is clear that Miranda was not in any way apprised of his right to consult with an attorney and to have one present during the interrogation, nor was his right not to be compelled to incriminate himself effectively protected in any other manner. Without these warnings the statements were inadmissable. The mere fact that he signed a statement which contained a typed-in clause stating that he had "full knowledge" of his "legal rights" does not approach the knowing and intelligent waiver required to relinquish constitutional rights. Cf. Haynes v. Washington, 373 U.S. 503, 512–513 (1963); Haley v. Ohio, 332 U.S. 596, 601 (1948) (opinion of Mr. Justice Douglas).[20]

No. 760. Vignera v. New York

Petitioner Michael Vignera was picked up by New York police on October 14, 1960, in connection with the robbery three days earlier of a Brooklyn dress shop. They took him to the 17th Detective Squad headquarters in Manhattan. Sometime thereafter he was taken to the 66th Detective Squad.There a detective questioned Vignera with respect to the robbery. Vignera orally admitted the robbery to the detective. The detective was asked on cross-examination at trial by defense counsel whether Vignera was warned of his right to counsel before being interrogated. The prosecution objected to the question and the trial judge

---

[20] *Hearing before the Subcommittee on Criminal Laws and Proceedures,* 1967, p. 43.

sustained the objection. Thus, the defense was precluded from
making any showing that warnings had not been given. While
at the 66th Detective Squad, Vignera was identified by the store
owner and a saleslady as the man who robbed the dress shop.
At about 3:00 P.M. he was formally arrested. The police then
transported him to still another station, the 70th Precinct in
Brooklyn, "for detention." At 11:00 P.M. Vignera was questioned by an assistant district attorney in the presence of a
hearing reporter who transcribed the questions and Vignera's
answers. This verbatim account of these proceedings contains
no statement of any warnings given by the assistant district
attorney. At Vignera's trial on a charge of first degree robbery,
the detective testified as to the oral confession. The transcription
of the statement taken was also introduced in evidence. At the
conclusion of the testimony, the trial judge charged the jury in
part as follows:

"The law doesn't say that the confession is void or invalidated
because the police officer didn't advise the defendant as to his
rights. Did you hear what I said? I am telling you what the law
of the State of New York is."

Vignera was found guilty of first degree robbery. He was
subsequently adjudged a third-felony offender and sentenced to
30 to 60 years' imprisonment. The conviction was affirmed without opinion by the Appellate Division, Second Department, 21
A.D. 2d 752, 252 N.Y.S. 2d 19, and by the Court of Appeals,
also without opinion, 15 N.Y. 2d 970, 207 N.E. 2d 527, 259
N.Y.S. 2d 857, remittitur amended, 16 N.Y. 2d 614, 209 N.E.
2d 110, 261 N.Y.S. 2d 65. In argument to the Court of Appeals,
the State contended that Vignera had no constitutional right to
be advised of his right to counsel or his privilege against self-
incrimination.

We reverse. The foregoing indicates that Vignera was not
warned of any of his rights before the questioning by the detective and by the assistant district attorney. No other steps were
taken to protect these rights. Thus he was not effectively apprised of his Fifth Amendment privilege or of his right to have
counsel present and his statements are inadmissible.[21]

No. 761. Westover v. United States.

At approximately 9:45 P.M. on March 20, 1963, petitioner,
Carl Calvin Westover, was arrested by local police in Kansas
City as a suspect in two Kansas City robberies. A report was
also received from the FBI that he was wanted on a felony

[21] *Ibid.,* p. 44.

charge in California. The local authorities took him to a police station and placed him in a line-up on the local charges, and at about 11:45 P.M. he was booked. Kansas City police interrogated Westover on the night of his arrest. He denied any knowledge of criminal activities. The next day local officers interrogated him again throughout the morning. Shortly before noon they informed the FBI that they were through interrogating Westover and that the FBI could proceed to interrogate him. There is nothing in the record to indicate that Westover was ever given any warning as to his rights by local police. At noon, three special agents of the FBI continued the interrogation in a private interview room of the Kansas City Police Department, this time with respect to the robbery of a savings and loan association and a bank in Sacramento, California. After two or two and one-half hours, Westover signed separate confessions to each of these two robberies which had been prepared by one of the agents during the interrogation. At trial one of the agents testified, and a paragraph on each of the statements states, that the agents advised Westover that he did not have to make a statement, that any statement he made could be used against him, and that he had the right to see an attorney.

Westover was tried by a jury in federal court and convicted of the California robberies. His statements were introduced at trial. He was sentenced to 15 years' imprisonment on each count, the sentences to run consecutively. On appeal, the conviction was affirmed by the Court of Appeals for the Ninth Circuit, 342 F. 2d 684.

We reverse. On the facts of this case we cannot find that Westover knowingly and intelligently waives his right to remain silent and his right to consult with counsel prior to the time he made the statement. At the time the FBI agents began questioning Westover, he had been in custody for over 14 hours and had been interrogated at length during that period. The FBI interrogation began immediately upon the conclusion of the interrogation by Kansas City police and was conducted in local police headquarters. Although the two law enforcement authorities are legally distinct and the crimes for which they interrogated Westover were different, the impact on him was that of a continuous period of questioning. There is no evidence of any warning given prior to the FBI interrogation nor is there any evidence of an articulated waiver of rights after the FBI commenced their interrogation. The record simply shows that the defendant did in fact confess a short time after being turned over to the FBI following interrogation by local police. Despite the fact that the FBI agents gave warnings at the outset of their interview, from Westover's point of view the warnings came at the end of the interrogation process. In these circumstances an intelligent waiver of constitutional rights cannot be assumed.

We do not suggest that law enforcement authorities are precluded from questioning any individual who has been held for a period of time by other authorities and interrogated by them without appropriate warnings. A different case would be presented if an accused were taken into custody by the second authority, removed both in time and place from his original surroundings, and then adequately advised of his rights and given an opportunity to exercise them. But here the FBI interrogation was conducted immediately following the state interrogation in the same police station—in the same compelling surroundings. Thus, in obtaining a confession from Westover the federal authorities were the beneficiaries of the pressure applied by the local in-custody interrogation. In these circumstances the giving of warnings alone was not sufficient to protect the privilege.[22]

The following case is particularly impressive in demonstrating that a defendant whose crime was well proved was freed on the basis of some questionable technicality.

In a six-to-two decision concerning a rape conviction in Mississippi, the Supreme Court said that the Fourth Amendment shields citizens against "the harassment and ignominy incident to involuntary detention." The ruling did not forbid police to take suspects to the station house without arrest warrants. But it said they are generally required.

Justice William J. Brennan, Jr. wrote in the majority opinion: "To argue that the Fourth Amendment does not apply to the investigatory stage is fundamentally to misconceive the purposes of the Fourth Amendment." He added: "I think it is high time this court, in the interest of the administration of criminal justice, made a new appraisal of the language and history of the Fourth Amendment and cut it down to its intended size.

[22] *Ibid.,* pp. 44–45.

"Such a judicial action would, I believe, make our cities a safer place for men, women, and children to live."

Associate Justice Stewart in his turn stated that fingerprints are not evidence in the conventional sense that weapons or stolen goods might be and should not be placed in the same constitutional category.

The ruling upset the conviction of John Davis, a 14-year-old Negro boy, for the rape of an 86-year-old white woman, Mrs. K. of Meridian. He had been sentenced to life in prison.

Yet Mrs. K.'s positive identification of him as the assailant presumably established the "probable cause" required by the Fourth Amendment as justification for taking new fingerprints. The reverse ruling was based on the fact that John Davis was kept at the police station one night for interrogation.

The Supreme Court also set aside the conviction of a Brooklyn man who set fire to an American flag. This somewhat hypocritical decision reflected the Supreme Court's attitude toward a "political" crime.

The five-to-four ruling found that Sidney Street, a bus driver, may have been punished for what he said rather than for what he did. And punishment for speech alone, however distasteful, said Justice John Marshall Harlan for the majority, is impermissible.

In another ruling, the Supreme Court warned anew that death sentences cannot stand if opponents of capital punishment are automatically stricken from juries.

It is entirely possible, said Justice Potter Stewart, that a person who has "a fixed opinion" against capital punishment or who does not "believe" in it might nevertheless be perfectly able to consider fairly the imposition of a death sentence in a particular case.

With that pronouncement the court directed a hearing in federal court in Alabama for a young Negro sentenced to be executed in the murder of a state conservation officer.

Numerous other cases of the permissive attitude of the Supreme Court could be recited. In all these cases there is a strange trend to protect criminals, to give them an opportunity to escape conviction. And there is distressing indifference on the part of the Supreme Court to the fate of the victim, as it was in the case of Mrs. K. No wonder there has been bitter and severe criticism of the Supreme Court's actions. This is evident from endless newspaper editorials, such as that of the *Post Herald:*[23]

> It is a fact that the worst crime rate in the nation's history has come during a period when many of the courts of the land—and in particular the Supreme Court—have erected unprecedented safeguards for suspects.
> Recent Supreme Court decisions, and subsequent lower court rulings based on those decisions, have made it all but impossible to gain a confession, or even to interrogate a prisoner.
> A minority statement in the report of the President's Crime Commission referred specifically to these two areas of police restriction, and asked if "the scales have tilted in favor of the accused and against law enforcement and the public further than the best interest of the country permits."
> Others are asking that question, in addition to just about every police officer. The burden of proof rests upon those who long have contended there is no relationship between punishment and crime.
> Never have the courts been so lenient, and never has crime in the United States been more rampant.

Or that of the Washington (D.C.) *Daily News:*[24]

[23] *Hearing before the Sub-Committee on Criminal Laws and Procedures.* Berkley, W.Va., March 28, 1967, pp. 285–6.
[24] *Ibid.,* p. 1190, June 18, 1967.

The U. S. Supreme Court has decided, six to three, that a New York state law permitting court-approved electronic eavesdropping is unconstitutional because it transgresses the Fourth Amendment ban on unreasonable searches and seizures.

This is an unwarranted ruling that takes another vital weapon away from those charged with enforcing our criminal law.

We agree with Justice John Marshall Harlan who concluded in his dissenting opinion that what the court did was "very wrong."

The court, by its ruling, Justice White wrote in dissent, "ignores or discounts the need for wiretapping authority and incredibly suggests that there has been no breakdown of Federal law enforcement."

He points out that while the majority opinion, written by retiring Justice Tom Clark, does not in so many words hold all wiretapping and eavesdropping constitutionally impermissible, it achieves the same result by "transparent indirection." Justice White attached as an exhibit the pertinent reports of the President's Crime Commission suggesting Congress enact a law that permits wiretapping with "stringent limitations."

Justice Hugo Black, another dissenter, accused the six-man majority with "being compelled to rewrite completely the Fourth Amendment" in order to strike down the New York law.

Supreme Court decisions in recent years restricting police power have aroused a great deal of controversy. More recently the Supreme Court made a ruling prohibiting police from stopping and searching individuals for weapons when they do not have enough evidence for arrest. This ruling seriously handicaps the fight against serious crime.

Apparently not all justices of the Supreme Court approve of its permissive trend toward crime and its too liberal interpretation of the Constitution. In his lectures at Columbia University law school, Justice Hugo Black said: "The courts are given power to interpret the Constitution and other laws, which means to explain and expound, not to alter, amend, or remake. Judges take an oath to support the Constitution as it is, not as they think it should be. I cannot subscribe to the doctrine that consistent with that oath a judge can arrogate to himself a power "to adapt the Constitution to new times."

"I strongly believe," said Black, "that the basic purpose and plan of the Constitution is that the Federal government should have no powers except those that are expressly or impliedly granted, and that no department of government—executive, legislative, or judicial—has authority to add to or take from the powers granted it or the powers denied it by the constitution.

"Our written Constitution means to me that where a power is not in terms granted, or not necessary and proper to exercise a power that is granted, no such power exists in any branch of the government."[25]

The most penetrating criticism of the Supreme Court rulings came from the Yale Law School's legal historian, Alexander M. Bickel.[26] According to Mr. Bickel: "Warren's Court strove to bring about the 'Egalitarian Society,' ignoring, "the heavy price [that] has to be paid for these occasional services to liberalism."

To achieve its egalitarian ends, Bickel argues, the Court played fast and loose with history, superimposed its values on the democratic process, tolerated injustice to individuals as a necessary if undesirable by-product of its efforts to remake the law, and ignored earlier and wise restraints on judicial policy making. The result was a peculiarly subjective quality to the court's benchmark decisions.[27]

Justice William O. Douglas adheres to a quite different position.[28]

According to him, we have in this country a revolution simi-

---

[25]Quoted from the article by James Kilpatrick.
[26]Alexander M. Bickel, *The Supreme Court and the Idea of Progress,* New York: Harper & Row, 1970.
[27]William M. Wiecek, *Saturday Review,* April 4, 1970.
[28]William O. Douglas, *Points of Rebellion,* New York: Vintage Press, 1970.

lar to that of our Revolution for Independence.

"We must realize," he writes, "that today's Establishment is the new George III." [p. 93] He is critical of and antagonistic to police. ". . . very often they arrest the wrong people. For the police are the arm of the Establishment." [p. 5] He is concerned about the activities of the Federal Bureau of Investigation, and he declared that the "FBI and the CIA are the most notorious offenders." [p. 31]

The lower courts often follow the permissive attitude of the Supreme Court regarding crime. Here is the case of an unbelievable court ruling.

On December 20, 1965, at 12:45 p.m., Policeman Thomas Jones observed two men carrying a large carton in North Philadelphia. There was something about the two men that aroused the officer's suspicion. The officer stopped the men for questioning and inside the carton was a large 17-inch portable TV set. After listening to their explanation of how the TV came into their possession and not being satisfied with it, the officer took the two men into custody.

Investigation was continued in police headquarters and at 4:25 P.M. the same day, John Maxwell, of N. 19th St. above Allegheny Ave., returned home and found his apartment burglarized and his 17-inch TV missing. Mr. Maxwell identified the television set the policeman had taken from the two men as his property, stolen from his apartment during his absence.

On the strength of the evidence presented before the magistrate there was little doubt as to the guilt of the defendants and they were held for the action of the Grand Jury. The Grand Jury found a "true bill" against the defendants and they were held for trial for court.

On June 30, 1966, the two defendants were brought up for trial before Judge David Weiss, of Westmoreland County, sitting as a visiting judge in the Philadelphia court.

The defendants' lawyer, from the Voluntary Defender's office, told Judge Weiss that in his opinion, this was an illegal arrest, basing this opinion on the grounds the officer had apprehended the two defendants before he knew a crime had been committed.

Believe it or not, Judge Weiss, after complimenting the officer for being so observant, agreed with the lawyer and discharged

the two defendants stating: "There had been no crime reported
at the time the men were taken into custody."

. . . Judge Weiss apparently had based his decision on one of
the many decisions which has been handed down recently by the
United States Supreme Court.

A decision such us this has given a license to steal, rob, rape
or murder with complete immunity, the only stipulation is that
the crime must be committed without witnesses or without
giving the victim the opportunity of reporting the crime.

"I wonder if the full impact of this miscarriage of justice can
be realized by the public," Mr. McDermott says.

"This may seem ridiculous, but the decision was made in a
Philadelphia court room based on, I believe, Judge Weiss' interpretation of recent U.S. Supreme Court decisions.

"I suppose the victim in this case, John Maxwell, should be
happy Judge Weiss did not give the thieves his TV set."[29]

Echoing the permissive attitude of the Supreme Court, an
American Bar Association study group recommended that the
maximum prison sentence for most crimes be set at five years,
a sharp reduction. Moreover, the ABA panel says, except for
such crimes as murder or treason, judges should have the authority to put the convicted man or woman on probation.

The parole system in this country seems to be quite permissive towards criminals. Edward C. Burks[30] reported that the
practice of paroling an increasing number of defendants prior
to their trial dates means that many of them are never tried at
all, according to Criminal Court Judge Amos S. Base. Crowded
court calendars are blamed.

Under the expanding parole system those defendants who are
considered good risks are released on their own recognizance
—"R.O.R." in courtroom parlance—after arraignment. In
other words, they are told to come back on a specified date for
a hearing or trial and they do not have to put up any bail. Many

---

[29] *Hearings before the Sub-Committee on Criminal Laws and Procedures,* pp. 1143–44.
The *Times* newspaper report by Thomas F. McDermott.
[30] New York *Times,* August 25, 1968.

other defendants are required to put up only a low cash bail—
$25 or $50.

The great majority of defendants arraigned in criminal courts
are paroled or released on a small cash bail payment before
trial. There is a trend, a Freudian trend, to believe that criminals deserve indulgent handling.

Recently the federal government accepted this permissive
attitude by classifying as "handicapped" persons with a history
of drug addiction and law violations, thus making them eligible
for special federal job training.

A spokesman for the Labor Department said that his department expects to handle a "minimum of 10,000 drug addicts in
the next 12 months." He noted that addicts "rarely go looking
for work" and must be "taken by the hand" to find jobs for
them after rehabilitation and training.[31] This unrealistic decision did not work.

One may see from the following case how American justice
works: Samuel Hemphill, 19, convicted of raping an 18-year-
old high school co-ed, was sentenced to 800 years in prison.

It was the second huge prison term handed down in the
Dallas–Fort Worth area in less than a month by juries concerned with law and order. Thus Joseph Franklin Sills, 50, was
sentenced to 1,000 years in prison by a Dallas jury February 26
for a robbery.

Hemphill's sentence was the longest ever given in the memory of Fort Worth prosecutors.

Despite the lengthy sentence, Hemphill will still be eligible
for parole in 20 years, and if he is a model prisoner, he could
be eligible for parole within 10 years after his sentence begins.

The state had qualified the jury on the death penalty.

The rape victim had testified during the trial that Hemphill

[31]Washington Associated Press office.

assaulted her three times. Angered by the increase in forcible rape, the jury sentenced the offender for 800 years. But, as we have seen, he might be free in a few years.[32]

We have given only a few examples of permissiveness exercised by our law enforcement system. We could recount many hundreds of cases which might shock any man with common sense. But one of the cases we mentioned briefly seems to us the most appalling case of injustice: the recommendation of the panel of the American Bar Association. This is an honorable association. The best lawyers belong to it. Some of them are conservatives, some liberals, and a few are left-wing radicals. They suggested that the punishment for crime should be reduced to five years with a liberal application of parole. They are ready to punish criminals for more than five years in only two instances of crime: treason and murder. Yet apparently they, the flower of our legal profession, gave no consideration to and did not say a single word about the forcible rape of women. If we properly understand the panel's resolution, rapists should be punished by no more than five years in prison, and this punishment should be reduced still more by parole. Thus we return to the beginning of this chapter when we protested against the silence on the part of our legal profession in regard to forcible rape. One might even say that there is a clear discrimination on the part of men against women.

"Poverty is not an excuse for crime," remarked J. Edgar Hoover. But is poverty the cause of crime? No statistical evidence has been offered by those who promote and defend this postulate. Perhaps there is still in me something of the concepts of the Russian intelligentsia, something that tells me that pov-

[32]Fort Worth Associated Press office.

erty does not necessarily predispose men to crime. In fact to state that it does is an insult to men who are not rich, who live modestly, who are near the poverty level. In Russia, the intelligentsia was proud to be poor. Physicians who were well-to-do were despised by students and other physicians. If we accuse a man of criminal tendencies only because he is poor, we question his integrity, his honesty, his dignity, his stability. The statement, promoted by our intellectuals, that poverty is the cause of crime indicates clearly their ultramaterialistic feeling. Basically they believe that poverty is a disgrace, that a poor man is a second-class citizen, that wealth means success, integrity, and honesty. *The paradox of this degrading and contagious attitude toward poverty is that it reflects the admiration for wealth and material success that has bedazzled our intellectuals. American intellectuals, in spite of their so-called liberalism, are the most materialistic group of persons in the world. And their campaign against poverty as the cause of crime is not only an insult toward the poor but distressingly hypocritical.*

They simply cannot understand that a poor man can be honest, happy, and satisfied with what he must live on. The world is full of poor yet happy men. In France millions of peasants exist on an income less than the one considered here as poverty stricken, yet there is little crime among them. In Soviet Russia one half of the population lives on an income far below the poorest persons in this country, yet there is no crime to the degree it is found in this country.

True enough, there are criminals among the poor as there are among more fortunate citizens in Soviet Russia—perhaps even more among the poor than the well-to-do. But many factors of a physical and psychological nature predispose a man to be a criminal, not merely his bank account, or his lack of one.

What do the figures presented in this chapter say? They say that forcible rape is not connected with poverty but a product of unlimited permissiveness; that murder and aggravated assaults are crimes associated with personal motivation or the act of professional criminals; that auto theft hardly can be linked to poverty; and that, in burglary, the most frequent crime here, whites outnumbered Negroes by two to one. These figures contradict the usual claims that the poverty of Negroes is responsible for their crime rate.

But the strongest rebuttal of the postulate that poverty is the cause of crime is found in the fact that millions of old and retired people who exist on a level close to poverty show almost no trend towards crime at all.

Crime, its problem and its origin, should not be approached from the assumption that its cause originated in poverty. This is a myth promulgated by sociologists and politicians. It is the individuality of a person, his inbred characteristics which make him a criminal or an honest man. His weakness, his self-pity, his permissiveness syndrome prepare the pathways to crime against society.

7.

Narcotics in America

• •

IN no other field, except the glorification of sex, is the influence of Freud on our young generation so strong as in the use of narcotics. "The services rendered by intoxicating substances," Freud writes,[1] "in the struggle for happiness and in warding off misery rank so highly as a benefit that both individuals and races have given them an established position within their libido-economy. It is not merely the immediate gain in pleasure which one owes to them, but also a measure of that independence of the outer world which is so sorely craved." In discussing the immense value of narcotics as a pleasure-inducing

[1]Sigmund Freud, *Civilization and Its Discontents,* London: Hogarth Press, 1927, pp. 30–31.

factor, Freud readily admits, "We are aware that it is just that property which constitutes the danger and injuriousness of intoxicating substances."

Almost overnight, in a short period of four or five years, this country—which had a small number of drug addicts in the past —became drug affected on a larger scale than in any other nation except in some parts of the Far East. Our country, at least a part of it, has been transformed from a healthy nation into a sick, confused, and greatly disturbed one. And here again, as in the case of crime, our liberal intellectuals, contaminated by Freudian postulates, have greatly contributed to the drug epidemic.

A variety of drugs are being used in this country. The most popular and widely smoked is marijuana. It appears that not only teenagers and adults, but children as well have become addicted to this drug, which is sold in various forms depending on its purity. The so-called hard drugs, heroin, LSD, cocaine, and others are gradually gaining larger distribution.

Marijuana: The Permissive Drug

Marijuana is the product of a plant existing for thousands of years and termed by botanists more than two hundred years ago as *Cannabis sativa*[2] (also known as Indian hemp). There are several various forms of resin present in this plant, which were described in Dr. Robert G. Walton's book.[3] Marijuana is a tall, annual weedy herb; the male and female flowers are on separate plants. Stems of the male plants yield hemp. The resinous exudation from the female flower clusters, and from the tops of female plants, yield the various products below:

---

[2]By Linnaeus in 1753. Otherwise known as Indian hemp.
[3]Walton, Robert G.: *Marihuana, America's New Drug Problem*. Philadelphia: Saunders Co., pp. 223.

Bhang: A decoction or a smoking mixture derived from the cut tops of uncultivated female plants. The resin content is usually low. Sometimes the word *bhang* is also applied to these inferior plants.

Marijuana: A Mexican–Spanish name for *bhang.* The term was originally confined to Mexico, and is the only one used for Indian hemp in America, except the vernacular of the streets.

Ganja: A specially cultivated and harvested grade of the female plants of Indian hemp. The tops are cut and used in making smoking mixtures, beverages, and sweetmeats without extraction of the resin.

Charas (also called *churus* or *churrus*): The pure, unadulterated resin from the tops of the finest female plants of Indian hemp, usually those grown for ganja. But in charas the resin is always extracted. It is known to us by the name of *hashish,* and from it is derived the drug known as *Cannabis indica.*

The preliminary findings by the National Institute of Mental Health after three years of study were included in a report released on April 4, 1970 by the House Select Committe on Crime.

The Committee concluded that marijuana traffic is at least an $850 million-a-year big business that is leading increasing numbers of young Americans into tragic lives—but that present stiff penalties are threatening respect for law in general and should be reduced.

It suggested a maximum one-week jail sentence for first-offense marijuana possession, during which the violator would be required to take a drug abuse education course.

"The growing drug culture," said Chairman Claude Pepper, Democratic Congressman from Florida, "is rapidly undermining respect for law and doing serious damage to the ability of the criminal justice system to safeguard the lives and property of the American people."

While marijuana helped boost all drug arrests 322 percent from 1960 to 1968—when 167,177 people were arrested including 43,200 under 18 and 6,243 under 15—the committee reported that judges jailed few of the young people because the penalties are unduly harsh.

On the basis of raw government estimates, the committee staff computed that six million people used marijuana in 1969 —600,000 habitual users spending at least $20 a week for a total of $624 million, 2.4 million spending at least $100 during the year for $240 million, and 3 million experimenters spending an insignificant amount.

The use of marijuana is increasing rapidly. In June 1970, Dr. Stanley F. Yolles, then director of N.I.M.H. reported close to 20 million users. By now these figures might have reached 25 or 30 million.

Sam Blum remarked: "Obviously, the N.I.M.H. figures rely on some wild guesswork, but no one at all awake throughout the last decade can doubt the direction in which they point. We Americans are using a lot more marijuana than we used to, and we will be using a lot more than that. It is now the very rare college student who has never tried the drug.

"In New York and the outlying areas where daytime New Yorkers go to sleep, high-school students complain that they must either smoke or learn to enjoy solitude. A ninth grader in Scarsdale High School estimates that 50 percent of her friends have tried marijuana and says that not infrequently it is smoked in the school ('like during fire drill, when we're jammed into the vestibule between the cafeteria and the outside door'). She knows of seventh graders in Scarsdale who are smoking; children in New York private schools are aware of its use in sixth grade. Juvenile-delinquency cases involving possession of marijuana get into the papers under datelines from Los Angeles to Hyannis Port."[4]

The most disturbing fact in this marijuana epidemic is that children also are becoming addicts to this drug. Marijuana smoking is widespread in our country. A dramatic case history of a 13-year-old girl was revealed by her father, a New York psychiatrist, Dr. Guillermo Salazar.

"The city is a jungle," said Salazar, who had appealed for public aid in effecting the return of his daughter, Isabel. Later he found the girl, and a police search was canceled.

Dr. Salazar called the drug problem (among children as young as 11, 10, even 8 years old) incredible, and said that in his own practice "teen-aged addicts had risen to 50 percent of all cases."

Backing Dr. Salazar's concern is a recent report by Governor Nelson A. Rockefeller's council on drug addiction. It found children from the age of eight years increasingly resorting to dope, often supplied by student pushers in elementary and high schools. The report claimed a 40 percent increase in drug arrests of 16- to 20-year-olds in 1968 over 1967.[5]

American newspapers and magazines are full of similar stories about young addicts. In Chappaqua, New York, five youths and one girl were arrested on a charge of possession of marijuana when New Castle Patrolman John Tondra stopped a driver suspected on drunken driving and searched the car.

The driver, David G. Bancroft, 21, was charged with driving while intoxicated and criminal possession of a dangerous drug. Police sent the contents of a plastic bag to a laboratory for weighing and testing. Possession of more than one quarter of

[4]Sam Blum, New York *Times Magazine,* August 23, 1970.
[5]Quoted from Arthur Everett's article, New York United Press International office.

an ounce of marijuana constitutes a felony, and the police said their first investigation indicated enough marijuana to justify the felony charge.

Besides the arrests in Chappaqua, numerous arrests were made in other towns of Westchester county. In White Plains 181 felonies were charged to the arrested drug distributors or users. In Mount Kisco and Bedford Village, localities where very wealthy families live, a number of arrests were made. Quite often the children of well-to-do families were involved in the use of marijuana.

Howard Samuels, Jr., 17, son of upstate New York industrialist Howard Samuels, was held for arraignment in Manhattan criminal court on charges of possessing hashish. The elder Samuels was formerly undersecretary of commerce.

The 19-year-old son of New Jersey Gov. William T. Cahill was picked up in Philadelphia and charged with possession of marijuana.

Harvey Fleetwood III, 25, son of a prominent banker and psychiatrist, prep school and college educated, has been arrested and accused of heading an international hashish smuggling ring that supplied college students in the New York area.

The ever-increasing use of marijuana and other drugs by American youth has gradually become a cause of great concern to educators, parents, and the public at large.

A Massachusetts poll conducted for the Boston *Globe* found that adults in the state were worried more about drug abuse among the young than any other state problem; 80 percent rated it a "very serious problem" with a greater emotional impact than inflation or crime in the streets. The fact that adults become so upset over drugs seems to make drugs more attractive to the young.

Surveying five California campuses, Richard H. Blum, a Stanford University psychologist, found that marijuana use had almost tripled in the 18 months ending in December 1968. In a new report, "Students and Drugs," Blum states that 57 percent of students at the schools had smoked marijuana at least once, compared with 21 percent a year earlier. About 14 percent were "regular" users, against 4 percent a year before.

"What we see now," says Blum, "is a rapidly increasing tempo. While it took approximately 10 years, by our estimate, for experimentation and use to shift from the older intellectual–artistic groups to graduate students, it took only an estimated five years to catch on among undergraduates, only two or three years to move to a significant number of high school students, and, then, within no more than two years, to move to upper elementary grades."[6]

Students of all ages are increasingly willing to experiment with marijuana. At many campuses, marijuana has passed the experimental stage and is an unremarked part of the social life. "Everyone does it," says a junior at one small New England college. "You see these complete Brooks Brothers straight arrows who turn on all the time."

"This is the view of dozens of educators and researchers, city and state officials, Federal health and law-enforcement authorities and students interviewed by The New York *Times* in recent weeks.

"Although authorities have watched drug use by teen-agers increase markedly here and throughout the nation in the last several years, many are alarmed by a casual and apparently fearless attitude about some drugs, especially marijuana, displayed by increasing numbers of teen-agers at increasingly younger ages.

". . . Marijuana is by far the illicit drug most widely used by teen-agers. It can be found in virtually all secondary schools in the city from exclusively private to overcrowded public institu-

[6]"Special Report," *Newsweek*, April 21, 1969.

tions. Most students who use it—and many who don't—consider marijuana no more harmful than alcohol and tobacco.

"Experimentation with marijuana has spread rapidly throughout middle-class and upper-class student bodies. Of 30 student leaders in the city's schools, more than one half said they smoked marijuana occasionally, and the remainder had friends who did. In the last month, four students at the exclusive Dalton School in Manhattan were placed on 'disciplinary probation' for using marijuana.

"Estimates of marijuana use range from 30 to 80 percent, with many students smoking it only occasionally. A survey of 100 Yale seniors found that 85 percent had smoked marijuana at least once; half smoked about once a week. A Barnard counselor notes an 'incredible' change in the patterns of drug use. The freshmen arrive 'sophisticated'—some have been 'smoking marijuana since they were 14 or 15.'[7]

New York City is the most permissive place in the United States, and its mayor, John Lindsay, is one of the most permissive mayors in our country. No wonder this city is an oasis for drug addicts and distrubutors, and that its schools are victims of this epidemic vogue.[8]

James P. Sterra reported the drug situation in New York City, covering various sides of this problem, with an emphasis on the use of marijuana.[9]

"The use of marijuana, has soared among students in the city's public and private high schools. It has reached the point where its open use, even in school buildings, is steadily growing.

"While a few of the more adventurous students smoke

[7] *Ibid.*

[8] A book entitled "Home Grown Happiness" is published in New York City. This book gives instructions on how to grow marijuana plants and all the technical details of how to extract the drug.

[9] New York *Times,* March 10, 1969. Since then, the use of marijuana in the schools of the city became much more wide-spread reaching proportions of a truly social epidemic.

marijuana in and around the school, most use it away from school. Student users classify marijuana with cigarettes and alcohol.

"Some school officials and students have noticed increasing drug use inside the schools, particularly in toilets and on staircases.

" 'Frankly, I think the problem is more widespread than most people can imagine,' said Edward R. Kolevzon, president of the New York High School Principals Association in the Bronx.

"For some students, marijuana use becomes a cheap, easy escape from school boredom, family problems and the range of questions they face while passing into maturity. In some cases school work suffers, emotional problems are exacerbated and other, more potent, drugs become a temptation."

More recently the marijuana-smoking epidemics have affected older, middle-aged Americans. Sam Blum reports that there is an increasing use of marijuana by older persons. He interprets this phenomenon in the following manner:

"Undoubtedly, the most important reason for the sudden outbreak of marijuana use in the adult working world is that young people have grown older. The pot-smoking art student of 1965 is the pot-smoking art director of 1970. The pot-smoking co-ed of last year is today's pot-smoking 'assistant buyer of better dresses.' And Seventh Avenue is adjusting to her.

"As she explains, 'You go into a showroom, and there's a straight set of salesmen for the old ladies, and they offer the old ladies a drink, but there are also hip salesmen, guys with real long hair and groovy clothes; and they just take you in the back and turn you on. In some of the houses the designers, the models, everybody is spaced out of his mind. And sometimes they lay dope on you. They're very cool about it. They come over while you've got your book out and you're writing orders, and they say, 'What do you do for kicks? Do you get high? I've got some very interesting stuff here,' and they give you an ounce.' "[10]

The marijuana-smoking epidemic has also affected the Army. Captain Morris D. Stanton, chief of the psychological section at Fort Meade, Maryland, told the senators he surveyed 2,372 men, ranging from private to lieutenant colonel, at a Cam Ranh Bay replacement battalion in November 1969.

About half of those sampled were entering Vietnam for the first time, and the other half were leaving it after one-year tours.

This was the major finding:

"Results showed that of the 994 outgoing enlisted men surveyed, 53.2 percent reported having tried marijuana at least once in their lives. About half these men—50.1 percent—reported using marijuana in Vietnam and 31.4 percent reported use before entering Vietnam.

"One out of six of the 994 was a habituated user in Vietnam —in other words he used it 200 or more times a year or more often than once every other day."[11]

How does marijuana affect people? As with all drugs or medicines there is always an individual response. Nevertheless there are some similar if not identical reactions in all who smoke this drug. Going through many described and reported cases, one finds that a boy or girl, either teen-ager or adult, has the feeling, 10 or 15 minutes after taking the drug, that they can do, and have the right to do what they want. Their self-control, whether strong or weak is considerably diminished. Their permissiveness syndrome is in full swing.

A 17-year old high school student recounted that after taking

[10]Sam Blum, "Pot-Smoking Is Not Just a Youth Kick," New York *Times Magazine,* August 23, 1970.

[11]Quoted from United Press International article in Tampa *Tribune,* December 3, 1970.

marijuana he felt "great." He and his friends broke the windows in their school. It was not a bitterness on their part. It was a show of their power. "I felt that I could conquer the world. I felt superior to my teachers, to my parents, without any animosity on my part. Driving a car—the highway belonged to me, only to me. I wanted to drive as fast as the car could go. It was a splendid sensation."

After smoking marijuana for two months, he noticed some difficulty in learning. "My memory was affected. I was unable to concentrate. I still am unable to concentrate in preparing for exams or reading a book."

A freshman in college, 18 years old, was considered by her parents a reliable, self-controlled, and highly considerate girl. Soon the parents noticed peculiar changes. "When Louise had a date," her mother would complain, "she would take my dress without even asking my permission. She never used to do such a thing before. She would argue with us, as if her father and I were ignorant nobodies. She became authoritative with us and with our friends. Soon she admitted without any regret that she was shoplifting. 'Why not?' was all that we got from her. Only then did we learn that she was smoking marijuana with the boy she went out with." The mother insisted that Louise was basically a good, warmhearted girl. There was no violence in her, or even temper. Yet an arrogance developed which had been absent before she became addicted to this drug.

The same manifestations seem to appear in almost every marijuana user: an inability to reason clearly; an intoxicating sensation of superiority; a decrease, at least temporarily, of intelligence; and a lack of self-control. All available data indicate that marijuana is actually a *permissive drug,* with all the side effects typical of the permissiveness syndrome. From this viewpoint one may understand the events and the riots and vandalism which occur in American schools, events which one tends to call revolution, but which are nothing but extreme permissiveness fed on the use or abuse of marijuana.[12]

Is marijuana smoking harmless to health?

Our liberal intellectuals claim that marijuana smoking is not dangerous to health and should be officially legalized.

Actually the vogue for the use of narcotics in this country received powerful support, some four years ago, from Dr. James Goddard, at that time the head of the Food and Drug Administration, which is empowered to fight narcotics.

He announced that marijuana is harmless, and there is no indication that it is dangerous to health to smoke it.

Goddard's remarks were addressed to an audience of students and faculty members of the University of Minnesota.

Goddard said it is true that people who have smoked marijuana have gone on to heroin and stronger drugs, but he added laughingly, it also is true that they drank milk.

"I believe the present penalty for personal possession of marijuana is too severe," he said. "Marijuana is not as dangerous as LSD, yet a person cannot be convicted of a felony for possession of LSD.

"A person can become psychologically dependent on marijuana, but then one can become psychologically dependent on any drug, including aspirin. Marijuana is not habit-forming," he said.[13]

Dr. Goddard also disapproved of imposing penalties for possessing the mind-expanding drug LSD. President Johnson wanted Congress to outlaw its possession, so when Dr. Goddard was summoned to give his views before the Senate sub-

[12]According to Norman Taylor's *Narcotics: Nature's Dangerous Gifts,* New York: Dell, Laurel Edition, 1966, P. 32, "some have charged hemp with being aphrodisiac, but there is no scientific warrant for this. . . . The plain fact seems to be that pure ganja has the reverse effect, and is taken by Indian priests to quell libido."

[13]Associated Press, Minneapolis, Minnesota, October 20, 1967.

committee on juvenile delinquincy, his superiors in the Department of Health, Education, and Welfare (HEW) quickly ordered him not to appear.

Calling for Goddard's resignation, Congressman Dan Kuykendall, Republican of Tennessee, told the House that Goddard "should be prevented from using the prestige of a high federal office to encourage delinquency and the smoking of pot by others outside his family."

Dr. Robert Baird, a prominent campaigner against marijuana and hard narcotics, decried Dr. Goddard's comments and also demanded his resignation.

Dr. Baird said Dr. Goddard's comments have done "irreparable damage across the college campuses as well as in the high schools."

"This man's knowledge of narcotics is notoriously poor," said Dr. Baird, who is director of a Harlem Narcotics Clinic. "Before he makes comments off the cuff, he ought to realize that 97 other nations who signed the narcotics convention of 1965, of which we are a part, can't all be wrong in realizing that marijuana is detrimental."

"I am surprised at him as a doctor," Dr. Baird said. "I am really mortified."

The Senate voted to sharply cut federal penalties for the use and sale of drugs, ranging from marijuana to heroin.

Under the bill, a college or high school youth picked up at a "pot" party would face a lighter maximum sentence than current law provides and could even escape without any criminal record.

The American Civil Liberties Union (ACLU) asked Congress to legalize the use and possession of marijuana.[14]

Lawrence Speiser, director of the ACLU's Washington

[14]New York *Times,* October 21, 1967.

office, told a House subcommittee the government has "not met its burden of demonstrating, through scientific evidence, that the use of marijuana is intrinsically harmful, causes antisocial behavior, or leads to use of stronger drugs."

It must follow then, he said, that "from the standpoint of social and legislative policy, marijuana, being no more harmful than alcohol or tobacco, should be given equal treatment with them."

Speiser said that while the ACLU is "opposed to the continuation of any criminal penalties on the use and possession of marijuana," it has no position on whether distribution should be legalized.[15]

Norman Taylor[16] is inclined to attribute no harmful effect from this drug. However, more recent scientific data indicate its effect on mental health.

A report was made to a House commerce subcommittee by Dr. Stanley F. Yolles, director of the National Institute of Mental Health, who in recent years played a key role in reversing the public belief that marijuana is a hard narcotic like heroin.

Yolles said that new studies, many of them conducted or supported by his agency, show that marijuana interferes with the thinking process and recent memory, weakens concentration, and "subtly" retards speech.

Marijuana was also found to stimulate anxieties and guilt feelings but, contrary to belief, it tends to turn a person inward rather than stimulate "conviviality," he said.

"Its sometimes pleasurable effects can be counteracted by considerable discomfort, dizziness, or sluggishness," Yolles added, and in high doses its active chemical constituent "causes psychotic reactions."

---

[15]United Press International, February 19, 1970.
[16]Norman Taylor, *op. cit., pp. 15–36.*

Although he reiterated there was "total agreement" among the scientific community "that marijuana is not a narcotic drug like heroin or morphine but rather a mild hallucinogen," he said the information available about it makes it "impossible to give marijuana a clean bill of health in any discussion on the continued restriction of its use."

Dr. Keith Yonge, president of the Canadian Psychiatric Association and head of the department of psychiatry at the University of Alberta wrote a memorandum which summarizes the substance of a report on marijuana.

Here are a few passages from Dr. Yonge's preliminary report:

". . . The use of this drug [marijuana] does indeed induce lasting changes in personality functioning, changes which are pathological insomuch as they impair the 'mental and social well-being.'

"The harmful effects are of the same order as the pathology of serious mental illness [psychosis], namely in distorting the perceptual and thinking processes and in diverting awareness from reality, impairing the individual's capacity to deal with the realities of life.

"The argument that marijuana is no more harmful than alcohol is specious. Although alcohol does constitute a serious health hazard in our society because of its readiness to intoxication, its action on the mental processes cannot be simply equated with that of marijuana. The primary action of alcohol is that of a relaxant. Impairment of mental functioning occurs when intoxicating quantities are taken. Marijuana, as with all the psychotropic drugs, on the other hand, acts solely as an intoxicant, its effects being primarily the distortion of perception and reasoning.

"In psychosocial development man grows from the prevalence of self-gratification and dependency, with little regard for reality, to the prevalence of self-determination and self-abnegatory involvement in his society. Against this progression, the trend toward 'instant' self-gratification and artificial self-exploration [by the use of psychotropic drugs] is distinctly regressive—a reversion to the immature, the primitive."

Dr. Julius Axelrod, a Nobel Prize winner and chief of pharmacology of the Nimb Laboratory of Clinical Science, declared that his study on human volunteers has demonstrated "that marijuana is not metabolized in man as quickly as it is in animals. It stays around longer in man. So the possibility of cumulate effect exists."[17]

All in all, there is very little doubt in the mind of objective scientists that marijuana is dangerous to mental health, even if consumed occasionally.

It is symbolic indeed that in our permissive society the drug which psychophysiologically induces and stimulates the drive towards permissiveness has become so widely accepted by our young generation of today, the adult generation of tomorrow. Marijuana has penetrated even into the elementary schools and nobody can foresee the harm which it would cause to our country, to our future generation of young adult men and women.

Heroin[18] *and LSD*[19]

A 17-year-old boy died of a narcotics overdose, the thirty-fourth teen-ager to die of drug abuse in New York City in 1969.

[17]United Press International, Washington, D.C., December 10, 1970.

[18]A white crystalline narcotic, $C_{21}H_{23}NO_5$, diacetylmorphine, a dangerous habit forming drug, affecting nervous system and liver. Cocteau, Jean: *Opium: The Diary of an Addict*, New York: 1961, pp. 1–202.

[19]LSD—lysergic acid diethylamide, the antagonist of the metabolite serotonin. Affects brain tissue, decreases intelligence, and ability to learn. Boris Sokoloff: *Carcinoid and Serotonin*, New York and Heidelberg: Springer–Verlag, 1968; J.H. Gaddum, "Serotonin and LSD," International Congress of Physiological Sciences, *20*:442, 1956; W. A. Frosh, et al., "Untoward Reactions to LSD Resulting in Hospitalization," *New England, Journal of Medicine*, 273:1235, 1965; "Adverse Reactions to LSD. Panic and Psychosis," *Medical World News, 7*:35, 1966.

Police indentified the victim as Peter J. Stergois, a known heroin user with a police record.

In one week, five teen-agers died of drug overdoses in the city. Last year, the city reported 900 drug deaths, 224 of them teen-agers.

Eight young men, four of them teen-agers, died over one weekend from using heroin, the New York City medical examiner reported.

The total was about average, but the percentage of teenagers was high.[20]

The New York City medical examiner's office listed the deaths in 1969 of approximately 220 heroin users under the age of 20, but said the figures are not complete. He estimated there are at least 20,000 teen-aged addicts in the city.

A 12-year-old boy was found dead of an overdose of heroin in the common bathroom of a Harlem tenement. An addict since the age of 11, his was the youngest drug death recorded in the city's history.

Fairleigh Dickinson III, a Columbia freshman, heir to a pharmaceutical fortune and son of a prominent New Jersey state senator, was found unconscious on the lower bunk of a friend's room on campus. He died from a combination of LSD and an overdose of opium he apparently had taken to "come down."

At some other schools, the use of LSD has crested. "Students got frightened by the walking wounded," says Dr. Richard H. Moy, director of the University of Chicago's health service.

---

[20]Associated Press, New York City office.

Commenting on Mr. Dickinson's death, a dean at Columbia said that there was "a massive amount of drug use" on the campus, and that it was "increasing each year as we get freshmen who have been exposed to it in high school and even junior high."

Drugs bring misery and tragedy to the young addicts. Such was the case of two lovers who killed themselves in Philadelphia.

A young drug addict awoke from a suicide attempt to learn his girl friend had killed herself.

"I'd like to be with Ann now," Smiler had said while recovering from the drug overdose. "Now that's she's gone, my life is shot."

Now Daniel Smiler, 23, has joined her. He hanged himself.

He was found hanging by his belt in a shower at Haverford State Hospital where he had been detained since the suicide attempt. His girl friend, Ann Barnett, 21, had died of an overdose of drugs at her home.

"My life has been with Danny and I could never start a new one after he died," she said in a note.

"Please forgive me for hurting you this way, but my life is over. Danny could not live with his habit and there is no way for him to get help any more," she wrote.

Ann's note to her parents said "We have tried everything and now that there is no way left. We will rest knowing that our love is so strong that it keeps us together always. We are sure that for us the end is really our own beginning."[21]

The harmful effect of LSD might result in violence. In Miami, the Associated Press reported that a young man shot

[21]Quoted from United Press International article in Tampa *Tribune,* Dec. 8, 1970.

a teen-aged boy and then fatally wounded himself after saying he was on an LSD trip and couldn't come down.

William Freedman, 22, died in North Shore Hospital where he had lain in critical condition for 12 hours with a bullet wound in the head.

William McQuilton, 16, was reported in good condition at Parkway General Hospital with a bullet wound in the right arm.

Investigators said Freedman went to a drive-in theater Thursday night to see McQuilton, an employee there. The two were talking in McQuilton's car parked near the front of the theater, and an argument ensued, police said.

Freedman said he was on an LSD trip "and couldn't come down."

Freedman pulled a .25 caliber pistol and, according to McQuilton, said, "I'm going to kill you and then kill myself."

The shooting followed.

The death of a 15-year-old girl from an overdose of heroin was disclosed with the arrest of the head of Harlem Teen City, a private community organization.

Edward Hamm, 34, was charged with homicide in the death of the girl.

Police said the narcotic, believed to be either heroin or cocaine, was administered to the teen-ager.

On the following day, the city medical examiner reported that eight males died from heroin over the previous weekend. Four were in their teens and the others were between 21 and 28 years old.

More and more cases of violence, murder, and suicide committed by addicts are being reported.

Fifty-one persons, including a mayor's son, were arrested in

Westchester County on charges of possession and selling narcotics, among them heroin. About 20 more were sought on
grand jury indictments and bench warrants. It was the largest
number of arrests ever made in Westchester for narcotics
offenses, according to Sheriff Daniel F. McMahon. The total for
the year reached 208, compared with 53 in all of the previous
year.[22]

In Coney Island, once a carefree playground for the city's
millions, three elementary schoolboys were arrested on charges
of selling heroin as an after-class occupation. Their ages—11,
13, and 15. Police said they cleared a total of $50 a day, while
their unidentified adult supplier collected $750 a day from
them.

The 59-year-old niece and 41-year-old grandniece of a former
Nevada governor were jailed on narcotics charges after a raid
which, according to agents, cracked the major heroin supply
ring for high schools here.

Arrested for possession of heroin were Lenora Pittman, the
niece of the late Vail Pittman, a Nevada governor in the 1940's,
her daughter, Ava, and a third Pittman girl, 21-year-old Paula
Linn Pittman, who refused to give her relationship to the other
two women.

Lt. John Sleeper described Ava Pittman as "the queen of the
heroin dealers for high schools here," allegedly earning about
$33,000 a week on 24 ounces of the drug.

He said the investigation has been under way since 1968. He
said it was learned that Ava Pittman usually traveled to San
Diego, California about twice a month. He also said agents
found documents linking her with an Arizona Mafia figure.

[22]New York *Times*, August 15, 1968.

Sleeper said that 15 minutes following the raid on the Pitt-man home—a fortresslike structure with iron gates and bars over the windows and heavy steel doors—agents raided a second home several miles away in connection with the same case.[23]

New York authorities say a father of four, arrested on drug charges, used teams of children to peddle narcotics.

Victor Santiago, 39, was taken before Judge Michael Ga-gliano in Brooklyn Criminal Court where Assistant District Attorney David Epstein said: "This man conducts a Fagin-like activity in the sale of drugs, using teams of children in these sales."

About 500 spectators in the courtroom applauded when Ga-gliano ordered Santiago held on $100,000 bail for a later hearing.

"If these charges are true," Judge Gagliano said, "then this man is worse than Jesse James. If they're true, he may have ruined the health and morals of children, and if any of them are addicted I think he should not spend a peaceful day the rest of his life."

Police said they found 14 decks of heroin, a quantity of marijuana, and equipment used in the narcotics trade in a Brooklyn basement laboratory when they picked up Santiago Thursday. They charged him with possession of narcotics with intent to sell.[24]

Hundreds of pages could be filled with newspaper clippings about the tragedy of drug use and distribution. The most distressing fact is that well-to-do families are involved in this disaster.

[23]Associated Press, Las Vegas, Nevada office.
[24]Associated Press, New York City office.

One of the most tragic stories was that of a young man from Salt Lake City who was addicted to LSD and recorded his torments and mental confusion before killing himself.

Craig Gardner, a handsome 19-year-old postal worker, got up early. He went to work for a few hours, visited his mother briefly, then went to his apartment and made a tape recording.

Then he drove from Salt Lake City to a remote area of Wyoming and, the county coroner ruled, shot himself.

The tape recording was found by a classmate and played at Craig's funeral—a rambling, touching account of a young man's struggle with the drug LSD.

"We hope to God it will help somebody else," said his mother, Mrs. William Blain of Salt Lake City.

Here is what her son said in his last hours:

> I can't think . . . can't think . . . can't think.
> Well, about all I have to say is—actually, the real reason is that I really don't know—[pause] I'll tell you one thing, Dave, [his roommate] and anyone else who's listening, you can really get messed up on that stuff.
> You might hear about it sooner or later, Mom—I'm sorry, Mom, Dad, and Bill—I'm sorry that your little boy has turned into an LSD addict.
> It's bad news—it really is. I didn't think it was when I was first taking it, but I've been getting pretty stoned lately, and you just don't know what's real and what isn't real. You really don't.
> All I can say is, I had to find out myself—kind of a poor excuse, you know—but I really shouldn't have taken any dope at all—any acid LSD—and I shouldn't really have started off with any grass.
> Marijuana, either. Of course, grass isn't bad—it's the acid that got to me.
> Tell you one thing—after you take so much of that stuff, you just really don't know where you're at sometimes. . . .
> I mean, I don't think I am, but what I've heard is that a person who thinks he's insane . . . or something would never admit it to himself. . . .
> I had enough problems of my own without even taking LSD to keep my mind bent. Well, actually what acid does is it intensifies everything to a great extent. This probably is what it did to me. . . .

All I know is I'm going to be in one hell of a fix when I have to face the Big Man up in Heaven. I'm not saying that with disrespect for the Big Man. I'm just saying it because I felt like saying it. And it says in the Bible that he who kills himself will not be resurrected. Well, this is the great punishment that I'm bestowing upon myself, not only physically, but, for what I've read, I'm going to be suffering eternally for this.

I have thought it over many times and there really isn't anything to live for. I don't think there is. And I really don't think anyone could convince me that there is—not me, anyway . . .

Then he drove to Wyoming and killed himself.[25]

Drug addiction, of heroin, LSD, and many other dangerous drugs, is growing fast and wide. It affects mostly the younger generation, and even preteen children. Yet all layers of our population seem to be contaminated by this gangrenous epidemic. It *is* an epidemic. And such a social epidemic could have developed and progressed so incredibly fast only in a permissive society.

The New York Bellevue Psychiatric Hospital reports a great increase in LSD addict cases, describing briefly the symptoms associated with or caused by this drug.

In addition to vivid, colorful hallucinations, the symptoms include many bizarre effects such as terror or other distortions of mood and perceptual distortions in which a patient may not, for example, be able to distinguish between his own body and the chair he sits in.

Some of the patients developed states of anxiety so powerful that the report called them "panic reactions." Some came to the hospital in the hope of getting relief from their drug-induced states of terror.

Others were brought in by friends who feared they would not be able to control the patients or prevent them from self-injury.

[25]Associated Press, Salt Lake City office, February 21, 1970.

Some of the patients came to the hospital months after taking their last doses of LSD because the symptoms originally produced by the drug were returning even in the drug's absence.

There are no reliable figures on the number of LSD addicts, but more reliable data are available on heroin addiction. According to the Federal Bureau of Narcotics, in a compilation for 1967, they gave the total figure of 62,403 throughout the nation and 32,347 in New York. Thus, appalling as it is, New York City seems to be the center of drug addiction.

"Heroin," *Time* reports,[26] "long considered the affliction of criminals, the derelict, the debauched, is increasingly attacking America's children. Part of the dread and the danger of the problem is that it spreads all too invisibly. No one knows how many heroin addicts of any age there are in the U.S. But in New York City alone, where most experts think roughly half the heroin users in the U.S. live, 224 teen-agers died from overdoses of heroin-related infections last year, about a quarter of the city's 900 deaths from heroin use. So far this year, over 40 teenagers have died because of heroin. There may be as many as 25,000 young addicts in New York City, and one expert fears the number may mushroom fantastically to 100,000 this summer. Cautious federal officials believe that heroin addiction below age 25 jumped 40 percent from 1968 to 1969. However imprecise the figures, there is no doubting the magnitude of the change, or the certitude that something frightening is sweeping into the corridors of U. S. schools and onto the pavements of America's playgrounds. It has not yet cropped up everywhere, but many experts believe that disaster looms large."

"A heroin epidemic has hit us. We must face that fact," says Dr. Donald Louria, president of the New York State Council on Drug Addiction and author of *Drug Scene*. Dr. Elliot Luby,

[26]"Kids and Heroin: The Adolescent Epidemic," *Time*, March 16, 1970.

associate director of Detroit's addict-treating Lafayette Clinic, concurs: "Addiction is really reaching epidemic proportions. You have to look at it as an infectious disease." Epidemic, of course, is a relative term, but as a Chicago psychiatrist, Dr. Marvin Schwarz, says: "Now we're seeing it clinically, whereas before we weren't. The kids on heroin all have long histories of drug use." At the California-based Synanon self-help center for addicts, the teen-age population has risen from zero five years ago to 400 today. In San Francisco, Dr. Barry Ramer, director of the Study for Special Problems, calls heroin now "the most readily available drug on the streets." He adds:

In my wildest nightmares, I never dreamed of what we are seeing today.

Heroin itself is a nightmare almost beyond description. By any of the names its users call it—scag, smack, the big H, horse, dope, junk, stuff—it is infamous as the hardest of drugs, the notorious nepenthe of the most hopeless narcotics addicts, the toughest of monkeys for anyone to get off his back. On heroin, the user usually progresses from snorting (inhaling the bitter powder like some deadly snuff) to skin popping (injecting the liquified drug just beneath the skin) to mainlining (sticking the stuff directly into the bloodstream.)

First there is a "rush," a euphoric spasm of 60 seconds or so, which many addicts compare to sexual climax. Then comes a "high," which may last for several hours, a lethargic, withdrawn state in which the addict nods drowsily, without appetite for food, companionship, sex—or life. Heroin, says one addict bitterly, "has all the advantages of death, without its permanence." After the high ends, there is the frantic scramble for a new supply in order to shoot up once again, to escape one more time into compulsive oblivion.

With an increased tolerance for the drug, he must use ever increasing amounts to reach the same high—thus the price of a habit can run as high as $100 a day. If he shoots too little, he does not get the kick he wants; if he shoots too much, he risks coma and death from an overdose. An overdose depresses the brain's control of breathing, slowing respiration to the point where the body simply does not get the oxygen it needs. If he tries to stop suddenly—cold turkey—he must endure the screaming, nauseating, sweating agonies of withdrawal.

The most tragic case was reported by the Wheeling (West Virginia) *News Register.* A soldier home from Vietnam less than a day confessed to his mother he was addicted to heroin and committed suicide a couple of hours later.

The soldier was given a clean bill of mental and physical health upon his release from the military this month, Don Daniels reported in the *News-Register.*

The newspaper gave this account:

His mother awoke in the middle of the night, heard her son stirring about and went to him.

"Mom, I'm hooked on heroin," he said. "It's like nothing inside me fits. Over there it's easy. It's like buying a pack of cigarettes. Anyone can get it. It's easy."

"Lots of guys are on it. Officers, enlisted men, lots of them. . . . It's so easy."

He shot himself a few hours after the talk.

"When we talked, he told me about it," she said. "I thought he was all right. We'd tell his dad in the morning and do something. But it wasn't all right, it wasn't all right at all."

"He would want others to know about it," his father said. "He was a calm kid . . . no trouble. It's lousy, all of it."

Even in Florida, a rather conservative state, heroin is making inroads among college students. Dr. Raymond R. Killinger of Fort Lauderdale, Florida stated: "We found that 50 percent of those taking heroin are habitually involved . . . and are in very big trouble."

The survey made in January 1970, he said, showed that more than 2,000 college students drop out of school each year because of the pressure of heroin addiction. Killinger said the habit costs $10 to $125 a day to support.

Questionnaires were sent to 5,000 students. Replies received from 1,747 of them qualified the report as one of the most comprehensive ever undertaken.

Killinger said heroin addicts were shown to come from "Strong, cold, paternalistic families"—most frequently from families of affluent business leaders and high government officials.

The survey showed that 34.7 percent of students have experimented with drugs—a far fewer number than most students apparently believe. Many students questioned reported "eighty percent" or "all of my friends" used drugs at one point.

Pressure from other students is the "major determinant of drug habits," and many nonusers may begin using drugs if they believe most of their colleagues also do. True drug usage on campus should be publicized, he added.

The survey indicated 24.8 percent of Florida's college youth have smoked marijuana; 7.3 percent experimented with LSD; 6.2 percent used mescaline or peyote; 5.7 percent used speed; 3 percent used cocaine and 3.7 percent used morphine.[27]

Thus we have the appalling picture of America today. According to the National Institute for Mental Helath, about 40 million Americans are involved in the drug addiction epidemic, or about 20 percent of the total population of our country. Children, teen-agers, and a good many of the middle-aged are using drugs. Men in the armed services in Vietnam, and in this country as well, are victims of this vicious epidemic. Besides marijuana which affects the health of its users, there is a variety of other drugs in addition to heroin and cocaine, equally dangerous to health, such as bath (barbiturates), bennies (benzedrine), blue angels (amytal), dollies (dotophine), meso (mescaline), meth (methadrine) and many others.

[27]United Press International story in Tampa *Tribune*, Dec. 18, 1970.

All these drugs, some more, some less, give a temporary pleasure gratification. All of them nourish and incite and increase the permissiveness syndrome. Many of them, the hard drugs especially and to a lesser degree marijuana, have an effect on mental activity and brain tissue which might be permanent.

So far the middle class and labor are not as much touched by the drug epidemic. But the upper class of America is deeply and widely contaminated by drug addiction. The sons of Robert F. Kennedy and R. Sargent Shriver were reported arrested on marijuana charges. Besides these two prominent men, numerous others have appeared in the news because their sons were arrested for using drugs: Senators George McGovern, Alan Cranston and Ernest Hollings; Governor William Cahill and former undersecretary of commerce, Howard Samuels. [28]

The Ivy League universities—students at Columbia, Harvard, Brown, and Yale—are among colleges reporting the highest incidence of drug use. The permissive attitude of upper-class parents seems incredible, and the liberal intellectuals are no less accommodating in this respect.

What is the origin of the drug epidemic? Why has this country, which only a few years ago showed no sign of this contaminating affliction, suddenly become seriously ill with drug abuse? Was this epidemic spontaneous? Autonomous and self-propelling? *We must reject this assumption without hesitation and doubt. The close relationship of drug promotion with the anti-war organizations, some of which are sponsored by communists, and the fact that it is directed toward the youth of our country and even more so toward the Army indicates, in my opinion, that a powerful political organization, probably communistic, is behind this drug promotion. Soviet Russia attempts to demoralize its enemies by various ways and means. In this case*

[28]Tom Buckley, New York *Times,* August 9, 1970.

they have achieved remarkable success due mostly to the permissive behavior of our society.

A few years ago, Dr. Timothy Leary, a radical and then an instructor in chemistry at Harvard University, caused a sensation and received extensive publicity by using his students as guinea pigs for experimentation with a dangerous drug, LSD.

There was nothing new about LSD. For a number of years it had been known as an antagonist of serotonin, naturally present in the organism, specifically in brain tissue. It was shown, long before Leary's publicity, that LSD neutralizes serotonin, and causes mental aberrations.[29]

But Leary declared that LSD is harmless enough to experiment with and that the exciting hallucinations produced by the drug were of high scientific interest. The work of Leary was received with much enthusiasm in radical circles which saw in it a new way to approach the drivings of the subconscious mind. However, some of his students became ill, and Leary was obliged to leave Harvard. Then he started the promotion of marijuana. He became known as the "high priest of pot."

In 1970 he was sentenced to 10 years in prison for smuggling marijuana from Mexico into the United States. Leary was sentenced by U.S. District Court Judge Ben C. Connally, who called him a "menace to the country" who "openly advocated violation of the law."

He was convicted January 20, 1970 in Laredo, on smuggling charges. He was held without bond at Santa Ana after a February 19 conviction of possession of marijuana.

Leary was first convicted in Laredo of failing to declare the marijuana for federal tax purposes, but the U.S. Supreme Court struck down the law under which he was arrested.

A retrial on the smuggling charge followed.

[29]Boris Sokoloff, (op. cit.)

Leary has been arrested at least 14 times in the past five years on drug charges. The only convictions have been in Texas and California.

Recently he escaped from jail and reached Libya safely, where he announced his intention to "destroy the U.S.A." He admitted his close relationship with militant organizations, specifically communists. There is no question that from the beginning of his drug promoting activity, he was backed by an organization which masterminded his escape to Africa. That was the beginning of the present drug abuse epidemic. The story of Leary proves once more, if such a proof is necessary, that the promotion of drugs is not accidental but sponsored and pushed by a political organization.

The fight, a successful fight, with the drug abuse epidemic is impossible unless public opinion backs it wholeheartedly. Such is not the case in our country. The liberal intellectuals who form and direct public opinion do not condemn drug abuse. An attitude of extraordinary permissiveness is in evidence almost every day. An article in *Weekend,* September 7, 1970, questioned the validity of evidence showing the harmful effects of marijuana. As with anti-war demonstrations, there seems to be an organized "public opinion" to legalize this drug. Fortunately, the U.S. Attorney General remains firmly opposed to the use of marijuana and remains unpersuaded of any good in legalizing the drug.

"To Mitchell, pot smoking is a symptom of immaturity, and he believes that youngsters are pressured into using it 'through a follow-the-leader chicken bit . . . to stay in the club.' He hopes that a national study commission on marijuana (similar to the Surgeon General's investigation of smoking) will turn up sufficient negative evidence about marijuana's effects to overcome that kind of pressure. 'It can be a dangerous and damaging drug,' he says. 'This is not my field, but in talking to people, I

think we'll find physical and chemical evidence of that. . . . If
we have a national commission to undertake a study and report
its findings, then we have two things—more information and
evidence that will be acceptable to the public.' "[30]

The growing epidemic of drug addiction in this country has
surpassed all similar phenomena in other nations. It menaces
the survival of the present young generation. It has caused a
dangerous demoralization of our nation. It requires urgent action to combat it with all possible measures.

[30] *Newsweek,* September 7, 1970, p. 22.

8

·

Sex in America

● ●

FREUD: *The greatest gratification man receives is sexual intercourse.*

We know all about sex, or so we thought. For the thousands of years of mankind's existence, all possible variations in sexual relations between man and woman were explored and used fully. It was generally accepted that nothing new could be offered or disclosed about this subject, old as the human race itself. All the perversions and abnormalities were explored during the centuries of the past. It was said that sixty-four methods of intercourse leave nothing to be added to.

Nations in the stage of decline and disintegration, such as ancient Egypt or the Roman Empire, were particularly involved in the extremities of sexual relations. But now it appears that we were wrong in our belief that nothing new can be offered to demoralized human beings. New horizons in the field of sex are proclaimed by young American radicals.

At my request I was introduced to Mr. X, the acknowledged leader of what is known as a revolutionary new sex movement. Formerly an assistant professor in sociology at one of the eastern universities, Mr. X is living in a comfortable apartment on the lower west side of Manhattan. In his early thirties, he is a handsome, tall, blondish man, with very long hair cascading down his back and shoulders, and a reddish beard covering a large part of his face and neck. He granted me an interview on the condition that his identity would not be revealed. His parents, still alive in Vermont, are conservative people and would be shocked by their son's revolutionary sex beliefs.

The goal of this new sex movement, I was told, is to annihilate The Establishment. It is through the liberation of man from all prejudices, inhibitions, rituals, false conceptions of man, and hypocrisy, that The Establishment can be more successfully and completely destroyed. It is in the sexual relations between man and woman that the bondage of both sexes is most in evidence. They are slaves of convention, of guilt feelings, of misery, more than in any other aspect of man's activity. It is in sex that the influence of tradition is overpoweringly repressive. The source of man's unhappiness lies in the repression of sex. "Complete liberation of man's sexual life is our revolutionary call," X almost shouted. Man and woman should return to the natural conditions in which primitive people have lived. Even more: They should return to the behavior of animals in which no repression of sex ever existed. Man should be engaged in sexual games as accidentally and freely as monkeys, or birds, or primitive tribes. When man experiences sexual desire he should take a woman, any woman who attracts him. The sexual relation should be simplified to a coitus, free from any restriction. The female should have the same freedom of sex. If she wants, if she is in need, she takes a man, any man, in fact as many men as she desires. She might change men as quickly as she pleases. "We declare absolute freedom of sex. We approve and advocate a mass sexual game, where continuous exchange of women and men might go on for hours, leading them to a nirvanalike state, to a supreme gratification of their inbred drive for happiness."

"And love?"

"Love is a product of our civilization. The new sex movement rejects love, or what is called love." Love, according to X, imposes a restriction on sexual freedom, and the freedom of an individual. Love is a sort of bondage. Yet friendship is admitted and welcomed.

"Nudity?"

"It's an essential part of our revolutionary sex movement. Why should the genital organs be hidden? The face is exposed, the genital organs are of greater importance than a man's face. The true freedom of sex cannot be separated from nudity. Clothes are a manifestation of man's hypocrisy."

"Is not the human body often ugly?"

"Nothing natural can be ugly. There is a beauty in ugliness, even in deformity. Even they must be accepted as they are. By covering one's body, human beings become victims of inner conflicts, of bitterness, and self-rejection."

"Do you realize the obstacles in your promotion of nudity, your rejection of thousands of years of mankind's development? From the origin of our civilization, man has tended to cover his body, especially his genital organs. Even the most primitive tribes, even cavemen covered their bodies with the fur of animals."

"That is not conclusive. They—men and women—covered

their bodies because of cold. True enough, with the progress of civilization, fancy clothes were created to please the vanity of both sexes, and to emphasize class distinction and often to hide the ugliness of the body. Sure enough, man must protect his body from the cold. But in sunny weather or in a well-heated house, at a party, nudity is imperative. I foresee a time, possibly in the near future, when hundreds of men and women will walk nude on Fifth Avenue, attracting no attention or criticism of the crowd. Is not nudity permitted in the intimacy of a bedroom? Why is it prohibited in public places or even at home?"

"Do you approve of pornography?"

"We despise it. It is the creation of a malignant mind, often of a sexually impotent man, who finds excitement in something he is unable to attain. No, our revolutionary sex movement is based on mental health, on a desire to avoid every and all suppression of our emotions."

"How do you recruit your followers? It is not easy to change the behavior of an individual with the background of his religious faith and the traditions of the society to which he belongs. A difficult task?"

"On the surface it appears to be so. In fact, however, believers, Christians respond more enthusiastically and wholeheartedly than atheists. There is nothing in the Christian faith which is opposed to nudity and freedom of sex. Their initial resistance to our credos is very strong. But once broken down, they are unreservedly with us. Catholic priests, nuns desert the Church and become members of our movement. Our method of recruiting neophytes is quite subtle. We advocate a collective confession. We call it 'searching our souls.' We invite them to a confession gathering of a few new persons, and several of our faithful members."

"Nude?"

"Not at this stage. All are in their usual clothes. Either my assistant or myself ask them to tell frankly, each one of them, about their repressed emotions and sexual desires. Once the newcomer starts to confess, he is predisposed to our next move. We explain that nudity is a symbol of freedom from the chains of civilization. We ask all present there to take their clothes off. The newcomers hesitate, some even resist, but at the end the whole gathering is completely nude. Once all of them are nude, we turn the discussion to freedom of sex. In most cases, the neophytes are not ready to obey our call to free intercourse. But after our members initiate the sexual game, gradually the rest of the gathering follow them. The new guests join our movement."

"Of what age are your followers?"

"Originally—they were in the late teens. Now more older men and women are coming to us. The late twenties, and early thirties. Often married couples; husband and wife both find a solution to their emotional problems with us."

"And hippies?"

"There is nothing in common between the hippies and our movement. They are weaklings, debased. Bored kids who look for superficial pleasure. Without principles or goals. They engage in sexual orgies but they take pot as well. We have a clear idea what we want, where we are going. We are liberating the human race from the aggravation imposed on a free man by civilization. Freedom of sex is to us a beautiful achievement in a spiritual sense. We are idealists. We promote purity for the sake of the free man."

This revolutionary new sex movement has aspects of a health cult. They do not smoke or drink, and there are no drug addicts among them. There is a cult of the body in their concept of life. They give much attention to various sports, such as swimming, tennis, and walking. Mr. X. insists that theirs is a regenerative movement. They pay a great deal of attention to their diet. In a sense they are not unlike the nudists of the past, but more vigorous, purposeful, and young. This revolutionary sex movement originated in Greenwich Village but its various affiliations extend to upper New York and New Jersey. They are organizing nudist farm colonies with a rigorous health regimen. The size of the following of this movement is unknown. They give no figures and in fact avoid all publicity. They enjoy life—there is no question about that. Although no word was said about Freud, some of his ideas apparently are incorporated in their beliefs.

In spite of the ardent conviction of the leaders and members of this sex movement that they can destroy The Establishment by promoting collective sex, there is no chance of their ever succeeding. As a friend of mine, a noted physician, once told me, he hates to see a woman, even a beautiful one, in the nude. "I see all the anatomical defects of her body, poorly formed bones, varicose veins, assymetric development of the muscular system. A nude body, young as it might be, attractive as it might appear when dressed properly, destroys all her sexual appeal for me."

From time immemorial, clothes have been created to hide bodily defects of both sexes and to create a mystery of the potentialities of artfully dressed persons. And, of course, clothes protect the body against cold and atmospheric changes.

Collective sex blocks the basic drive of every human being to love and to be loved, which is based on the inbred desire of almost all individuals to achieve long lasting intimate relations between man and woman. Nudity has been accepted for thousands of years as the privilege of such an intimate relationship.

Collective sexual intercourse is common among American youth and is more prevalent than many suspect. Both nudity and collective sex are practiced in many hippie camps. But there is no overt ideological significance attached to hippie manifestations as is the case of the revolutionary new sex movement. In the case of the hippies, it is a sign of demoralization, like their general lack of cleanliness, long hair and beards, dirty clothes, and unhygenic way of living. As one young girl of a hippie camp declared proudly to a reporter, she was pregnant but she did not know who the father of her forthcoming child was. She had purposely had intercourse with three men at the same time.

Communal living is a frequent phenomenon in America to-day. The commune movement even has its own journal: *Modern Utopia.* According to Herbert A. Otto, marriage counselor,[1] this journal is issued by the Alternatives Foundation of Berkeley, California, and is in its fourth year of publication. In 1969, this journal published the first comprehensive directory of intentional or utopian communes in the United States and the world. It lists the addresses of almost 200 intentional communities in this country. California leads the directory with more than 30 listings. New York has 28 and Pennsylvania 13, with communes listed in 35 other states.

A number of communes are deliberately organized for the purpose of group marriage. However, the concept of group marriage differs widely. Some communes exclusively composed of couples have a living arrangement similar to the "big family" or group family that originated in Sweden in 1967. These married couples share the same home, expenses, household chores, and the upbringing of the children. Infidelity is not encouraged. Other group-marriage communes tolerate or encourage the sharing of husbands and wives. At the other end of the group-marriage continuum are communes such as The Family near Taos, New Mexico. This group of more than 50 members discourages pairing—"Everyone is married to everyone. The children are everyone's."

The life span of many communes is relatively short due par-

[1]Herbert A. Otto, "Has Monogamy Failed?" *Saturday Review,* April 25, 1970.

tially to disagreement over household chores or work to be performed. This is a major source of disruption. When members fail to fulfill their obligations, disillusionment and demoralization often set in. Closely related are interpersonal conflicts, frequently fueled by the exchange of sex partners and resultant jealousy. Drugs do not seem to create a major problem in most communes, as there is either a permissive attitude or drug use is discouraged or forbidden.

Collective or group confession is quite popular in New York and other large cities. Some of these groups are openly Freudian, such as the group therapy conducted by psychotherapist Samuel Slavson.[2] Although he is not an analyst, his orientation is Freudian. The confessions of participants are highly emotional and often violent. They always relate to sexual activity and gradually create an atmosphere of high sexuality in the group room. While the group therapy conducted by Slavson is ethical, nudism is advocated as a basis for more complete mass confession in some less ethical group therapies.

The attitude toward extramarital sexual relations has greatly changed in America during the last decade. Sexual freedom has gradually penetrated not only the upper class, where there always was a tendency in this direction, but it is becoming more evident among the middle-class married population.

A demonstration such as this one which recently occurred in San Francisco[3] could not have taken place some years ago:

A group of young ladies, who said they were "sex-starved," protested on behalf of guilt-free adultery.

The demonstrators held a bedsheet banner aloft calling for "successful adultery for the happily married man" during a

2 *Time*, December 1969.
3United Press International, San Francisco office.

unique demonstration in the city's financial district.

"Married men should spread their favors around more evenly," Cecily K. told the crowd that gathered around her.

"Admit it to yourself. You do commit adultery, anyway," she told the gentlemen in the audience, most of them married. "Do it right. Do it without hangups."

Mrs. K. commented that she felt her own marriage would have been saved had both participants been able "to do away with selfish, possessive love."

She said that she wouldn't have felt jealous if her husband had strayed. "Why should I? As long as a wife gets her share of love, why should she begrudge her husband an extra measure of happiness?"

After all, she pointed out, two can play the game.

"Women are more romantic and just as erotic as men," she said. "They love being made love to on the grass on a sunny afternoon—when their husbands are at work and another eligible male could help out."

The bitter truth about this demonstration is that numerous married couples of all ages would fully agree with Mrs. K.'s statement.

Sex has burgeoned on campuses and at schools. Surveys conducted in 1959–60 indicated that only 15 to 18 percent of co-eds, depending on the type of college or university, admitted to having sexual relations with males before marriage. A survey conducted in 1969 painted a different picture: as many as 80 to 85 percent of co-eds approved of sexual intercourse with males. They considered such behavior normal and desirable. Some of those who remained virgins during their college years, complained that they simply had no opportunity—regrettably, they said.

Yet there is an indication that narcotics, particularly

marijuana, are partially replacing sexual activity among college students.

The use of drugs has become so predominant among college students that it has relegated sex to second place, according to a survey on drug addiction made by the Essex County New Jersey Council.[4]

Students express a certain boredom with sex, said Dr. Sylvia Herz, a psychologist–sociologist of South Orange and chairman of the council: "since sex is easily attainable, available, taken for granted, and has lost its yesteryear spirit."

Dr. Herz disclosed the findings of six months of research in which 150 students of both sexes were interviewed in three colleges in New York and New Jersey. She would not identify the colleges.

The use of drugs and sex appear to go hand-in-hand, however. "Of those tested, in all cases where a student had experimented with drugs, he, self-admittedly, had also participated in the sexual act at some time."

Of the students tested, 42 percent said they had sexual relations "often," 19 percent "very often," 31 percent "a few times," and 8 percent "never."

Although more than one quarter of those interviewed had used marijuana and amphetamines, which are stimulants, at different times, the interviewees felt that about 50 percent of the student body used marijuana.

The figures of 85 to 92 percent of students who engage in sexual relations in colleges in the North are higher than the national figures—75 to 80 percent. In 1966, there were about 90,000 unwed teen-age mothers in this country, an increase of 100 percent in 10 years.[5] These figures almost doubled for 1969.

---

[4]United Press International, Newark, New Jersey office.
[5]John Kobler, "Sex Invades the Schoolhouse," *Saturday Evening Post,* 1966.

"One out of every three brides under 20 goes to the altar pregnant. Estimates of the number of illegal abortions performed on adolescents run into the hundreds of thousands."[6]

With the laxity of sexual intercourse, or what we call sexual freedom, American youth is confronted with a new danger: venereal disease is reaching epidemic proportions. According to the report of the U. S. Public Health Service, 529,575 cases of venereal disease occurred in 1969, and about 33 percent of the cases were teen-agers.[7]

Not many years ago, health authorities looked upon venereal disease as a problem under control and on the way toward elimination. Today, venereal diseases are sweeping widely through America.

Syphilis now ranks as the No. 2 killer among communicable diseases, surpassed in deadliness only by tuberculosis.

Both syphilis and gonorrhea are highly contagious. They are called venereal diseases because they are spread primarily—in fact, almost exclusively—through sexual relations. Both are curable, but the cure is getting more difficult because of the appearance of new strains of the disease resistant to antibiotic drugs.

Health authorities attribute the rising incidence of venereal disease to several factors:

—The age distribution of the population has shifted, with a much higher proportion now concentrated in the 15 to 20 age group which has the highest rate of extramarital sexual activity.

—Greater permissiveness in moral codes, and the availability of contraceptive pills, have resulted in an increase in casual sexual encounters.

—People have been lulled into a false sense of security by the

[6] *Ibid.*
[7] Louis Cassels, United Press International Senior Editor, April 15, 1970.

widely-held but mistaken belief that modern antibiotics offer a quick, easy, surefire cure for venereal disease.

Reports of the U. S. Public Health Service contradict many other popular notions about venereal disease.

The commonly held idea that venereal diseases are much more prevalent among servicemen than civilians is not borne out by official reports, which indicate that the rate of infection in the military closely follows the national trend for civilians of the same age group.

From the college campuses, sex has descended to the secondary and primary schools. Even in communities which are quite conservative, pregnant pupils are a frequent phenomenon. Charles Hendrick[8] reported the results of the survey conducted by Florida State Senator de la Parte on illegitimate births.

The report stated that, of all births in the state in 1969, 14 percent were illegitimate.

A county-by-county breakdown, accompanied by reports concerning married and unwed mothers attending schools, tells us, for instance:

Of 1,026 illegitimate births in Hillsborough County in 1968, 452 unwed mothers were from below age 15 to age 18. Thirty-four were under 15; 60 were 15; 106 were 16; 126 were 17; and 126 were 18 years old.

School-age girls that year accounted for a full 40 percent of total illegitimate births.

Hillsborough County, according to a school official, follows much the same pattern as the state of Florida. In 1968, 41.5 percent of 14,529 illegitimate births were to mothers of school age, under 15 to age 18. The figure is expected to be considerably higher for 1969.

[8]Tampa *Tribune*, April 16, 1970.

A survey concerning the reaction of school pupils to sexual intercourse brought out the most dramatic results. As an example, the poll conducted at the New Lincoln School in New York City revealed that eleventh graders—77 percent—found nothing wrong with premarital intercourse. Similar polls taken in dozens of other schools gave similar results: 70 to 75 percent. Not only did eleventh or tenth graders approve of premarital sexual intercourse, but even eighth and ninth graders were not reluctant to participate in sexual games.

The information shown by the polls aroused the anxiety of parents and teachers. And, first in New York City, so-called school sex education was initiated. This soon resulted in a national controversy.

The Freudian influence is well pronounced in the campaign for sex education. Since Freud's major postulate was that children as young as six to seven years of age are sexually conscious, sex education has been directed toward younger pupils. California was one of the first states to organize sex education on a large scale.

John Kobler[9] vividly described the methods used in San Diego. A team of two men and three women, social counselors, were hired to promote a "wholesome attitude toward boy–girl relationships." The team circulated among 31 secondary schools of the city. A special film was produced to educate children about sex. Mrs. D. gave the demonstration of the film to 40 girls in the ninth grade class. Her listeners were predominantly white, girls between the ages of 12 and 14.

"You are going to see how a boy feels after intercourse with a virgin," Mrs. D. said in her introduction.

"Pay lots of attention to the game they're playing," Mrs. D. continued. "Do you know why they're playing it? And listen

[9]John Kobler, *op. cit.,* pp. 23–24.

carefully to the words they use. 'Cherry' means what we call the hymen. That's what the boys in the film are referring to. You'll also hear one of them say, 'Did you bounce her high?' Not all boys talk or feel that way. Often the boy who talks big is insecure about his masculinity."

Lights out. Music. Peter, a high-school senior, who brags about his prowess as a seducer, is challenged by his companions to prove it. Let him try his wiles on his virginal classmate, Nicky. At first Nicky resists. But gradually she succumbs to flattery. Her downfall occurs in the back of a car borrowed from Peter's father. Afterward Peter, conscience-stricken and ashamed, avoids Nicky. She grows resentful and angry at herself for having ignored her girl friends' advice. Hadn't they warned her that Peter would drop her once he "scored?" The film ends with Peter's cronies vicariously enjoying his adventure.

During the remaining 20 minutes of class Mrs. D. leads a "buzz session" about the moral implications of *The Game*. "Now what was really going on? Yes, Judy."

A blue-jeaned 14-year-old, her blond hair tumbling to her waist, ventures: "He didn't really want to go through with it."

Counselor beams. "Precisely. I've talked to boys who told me, 'I was hoping she'd say no.' "

Second girl: "I don't think that Nicky was really so innocent."

Mrs. D.: "How many among you think she was enjoying the game? [Up go some 30 hands.] You remember when Peter phones and asks, 'What are you doing?' and Nicky tells him, 'I just got out of the tub.' She wanted him to picture her in the nude, didn't she? 'I'll be right over,' he says. Then she plays coy. 'Is that nice?' When he does arrive, why should she receive him in her bedroom, with her parents absent? Eventually she falls for the oldest line, 'You're laughing at me,' Peter says.

She has to show him she takes him seriously. . . ."

Also in San Diego, a 13-year-old eighth grader L. who saw the film in another school, arrived home one evening and told her mother she had had intercourse with a boy of 16. Her mother was horrified, asking her why she had done such a thing. "I wanted to see if the movie was right. . . . It was."

John Leo of the New York *Times* tells us about the fight over sex education in New York and elsewhere.

"Like many liberals, Barbara S. assumed that objections to sex education programs were confined to the right wing.

"But recently her 11-year-old son reported that a classmate refused to return to school after he had been asked to tell his class what a eunuch is. Later her 6-year-old daughter, shocked at seeing her class's hamsters devour their young, drew picture after picture of parents eating their babies.

" 'Now I'm very nervous about these programs,' said Mrs. S., a science writer and the wife of a Manhattan psychiatrist. 'If this sort of thing can happen in two of the best schools in the country, it's hard to think what might be going on in schools that aren't so good.' "

Sex education programs, which are now given in half the country's public and parochial schools, have been under fire from political conservatives as "raw sex." Now these conservatives are being joined by an increasing number of liberals, such as Mrs. S., who believe the programs are haphazard and ignore developments in child psychology.

Sex education varies from school to school, but generally the children in kindergarten and the first five grades are taught the basic facts of reproduction and those in grades six to nine are told about dating behavior and the physical and emotional changes of puberty. In the higher grades, discussion usually centers on the psychological and moral aspects of sex.

In New York City, 70,000 pupils in 320 public schools receive sex education as part of an experimental project. A representative of the Roman Catholic Archdiocese of New York said
that the chancery had endorsed sex education in the city's
parochial schools, but had not yet set up classes.

Sex-education programs were introduced, in part, because of
concern over sex ignorance, illegitimate births, venereal disease,
and divorce. They have the support of committees of the National Education Association and the American Medical Association and state and national Parent–Teacher Associations.
But the methods, materials, and people employed have led to
deep concern.

Speaking of the incident in her son's class, Mrs. S. said:

"At the age of 11, many boys are undergoing castration
anxiety with the onset of puberty. It's exactly the wrong time
to be forcing them to think about eunuchs."

Dr. Rhoda Lorand, a Manhattan analyst who treats children,
has become a crusader against the programs. She agrees with
Mrs. S. "What they are giving the children is grossly inappro-
priate at every level, from kindergarten through high school,"
she said.

"They" are local community groups in all 50 states, usually
made up of parents, clergymen, and psychiatric personnel. The
dominant national organization that aids and guides local
school programs is SIECUS—the Sex Information and Education Council of the United States which is headed by Dr. Mary
S. Calderone, a former medical director for Planned Parenthood.

There are many pro and contra voices about school sex education. Father Jean Blais of Mount St. Paul College in Wisconsin is enthusiastic about sex education. To him a thoroughgoing
school sex education program is an important part of a youngster's growing up. Father Blais teaches such course at his col-

lege. He laments the public controversy that tries to push sex education back into the gutter.

"Sex education is not just information," he says. "It's proper attitudes. We teach kids everything else, but [we] don't teach them about themselves."

Father Blais agrees that the responsibility for sex education belongs to the family. But he points out that scarcely one in five children receives any such information from their home. "Most receive sex education from their friends," he adds.

California state superintendent of public instruction, Max Rafferty, in his column "Who Needs More Sex Education?" wrote: "How can the schools unilaterally solve a problem which originates outside the schools and which permeates society as a whole? . . . And the answer is: They cannot. Only when we adults . . . set a decent example and demand decent behavior from the young will children start growing up to become the kind of people we want them to be, and should have been ourselves."

The most incisive comment on the subject comes from Prof. Ernest Van den Haag of New York University, who observes that what most sex education courses are bent upon teaching is the kind of thing no one need seriously worry about, because our children will find out all about it on their own.

The principal organized lobby for sex in the schools, SIECUS, is very aggressive and pushes its plans with great energy.

Fred Ganas, director of the Seminole–Duval–Bartow sex program, said naively that it has been very successful.

"The kids are crazy about it. The reaction of the students is outstanding. They're saying that this is the first course where they've really been involved."

As was said, school sex education varies from state to state. A California group opposed to sex education says conservatively that at least 50 percent of the state's children are getting what it calls, "courses in pornography," but a state official estimates only 20 to 25 percent of the state's 1,200 school districts have "true sex education."

All 40 school districts in Utah have a state-recommended "maturation education" program, described as a mild form of sex education.

Every public school in Hawaii is included in a statewide sex education program in effect since September 1968. It has two phases, one aimed at fifth and sixth grade students and the other at tenth to twelfth graders.

A study by Central Washington State College indicates that 90 percent of secondary schools in that state have some kind of sex education. Nearly all offerings are elective, the study found, and the ratio electing to take them is 20 girls to each boy.

In Oregon a legislative contest developed over bills both to compel school districts to introduce sex education and to prevent them from doing so. Meanwhile a state official estimates that 60 percent of the state's school children are getting sex education in 40 percent of the 400 districts—including the big areas of Portland, Salem, and Eugene.

Kansas reports 1,015 of 1,362 schools have some form of sex education, Minnesota 300 out of 450 schools districts, and Iowa 399 out of 453 districts.

Sex education offers many variations to the educators excited by the new pathways of promoting Freudian happiness.

A teacher in a private school came up with a highly individualistic and impromptu technique. When a young married teacher at Shady Hill, a Cambridge, Massachusetts day school (400 boys and girls, ages 4 to 14) reached the visible stage of pregnancy—to the fascination of her five-year-old pupils—she began to use her own unfolding experience to explain human reproduction to them in very personal terms.

The University of Nevada organized "Sex Week," so named by its sponsors, the Associated Women Students, and included films on sex education and a university health department presentation on birth control, planned parenthood, and premarital sex.

"These are timely and contemporary topics we are interested in," said the vice-president of the Associated Women Students. "I am not certain we have all the facts about them."

The discussion of lesbianism was led by Rita Laporte, president of the Daughters of Bilitis, a San Francisco-based organization which defends female homosexuality.

A show was staged in the campus gymnasium by members of Messiah's World Crusade, a communal group that travels with band, chorus, and speakers to spread its message.

No less novel was the education in sociology introduced by Dr. Donald Robertson and Marion Steele, assistant, at California State College at Long Beach.

Nude men and women were demonstrated to students at the lectures. The teachers stated that they are fighting American prudishness. One can expect many other variations in sex education in schools and colleges.

What can be said, what comment can be made about the new American vogue in the field of sex: sex education in secondary and primary schools? From the examples quoted there seem to be quite different concepts of what should be accomplished by such an education in various states and communities. To a Frenchman or Italian or Spaniard, this new vogue would appear a mental aberration on the part of our intellectuals. In the majority of European countries, including those behind the Iron Curtain, the idea of sex education in schools would appear ridiculous. For there youth learns about sex when the time arrives to start it in practice.

Let us first speculate as to what the purpose of sex education is. There are two possibilities, two quite different purposes. If we want children to learn about sex, anatomically speaking, this subject should be part of a course on biology. It should be presented as all other topics of biology are taught, without emotional curiosity being aroused in the pupils. But if we judge the goal of this sex education by the film demonstrated at the San Diego schools, we must admit that the initiators of this vogue intend to teach or to show pupils how *a boy and a girl achieve intercourse.* Since the majority of social workers are Freudian followers, one may assume that they actually would like the pupils to employ their sexual opportunities at an early age.

Another question: Why do the initiators of this movement believe that girls and boys of 13 or 14 or even earlier are as innocent as youth of the same age some decades ago? The polls and surveys briefly mentioned above seem to suggest that the youth of 12 to 15 know as much about sex as their teachers. Still another question of major significance may be asked. Would sex education in schools decrease the sexual curiosity of pupils and would it prevent an increase in sexual intercourse among school age youth? There is no reason to believe that such will be the result of sex education. On the other hand, if there is no sex education in schools, there is no hope that the pupils will be more reserved in their sexual activity.

One may conclude that there is no difference whether or not sex education in schools is applied. In both instances the result will be the same. Tragically enough, the secondary schools will follow the colleges in their practice of sexuality as they have in smoking marijuana. If we cannot stop the use of narcotics, we cannot stop the progressing sexual activity. For our children live in an extremely permissive society. They witness every day the permissive attitude of their parents, teachers, and administrators, in all aspects of life in this country.

The by-products of the freedom of sex movement are pornography and obscenity. There is nothing new in them. For decades one could buy pornographic photos and drawings in almost every bistro of Paris, Rome, and other European cities. A shabbily dressed man would approach you while you were drinking your beer and would offer you a collection of dirty pictures. Middle-aged tourists, tired of the monotony of their married life, would pay a few francs for the treasury they would bring home and show their male friends and business acquaintances. In the Paris and Marseilles *boîtes de nuit* one could see all kinds of sexual obscenity, if he liked this sort of cheap excitement. However, there is a considerable difference between the long-existent European obscenity and pornography and those which are mushrooming in this country.

The radical intellectuals declare that American pornography and obscenity are part of the revolutionary movement, the goal of which is to destroy The Establishment. Moreover, American pornography and obscenity are bringing in enormous amounts of money to "idealistic" intellectual authors and playwrights as well as to unscrupulous publishers and play producers.

Yet the American public, we are told, should be tolerant of the promoters of pornography and obscenity in this country. Their engrossment in these deviations from normal sexuality indicates, according to Freud,[10] that they are in a state of well-advanced sexual neurosis, sexual psychopathy, or impotency. They should not be persecuted, these American promoters of obscenity. They should be treated. One arrives at such a conclu-

[10]Sigmund, Freud, *Three Essays on the Theory of Sexuality,* London: Imago Publishing Co., 1949.

sion after reading their books and seeing the plays produced by them. They call the pornographic movement the new eroticism which, according to them, has liberated Americans from prudishness.

The new eroticism is closely associated with sexual nudity. This term is applied to the exposure of sexual organs and emphasizes their manipulation. There is nothing wrong with nudity when an artist paints a nude woman or man without focusing particular attention on their genitals. But sexual nudity is a pathological phenomenon, a morbid condition, which is often called the nudity syndrome. Numerous cases have been described in the medical annals of women who undress themselves in public and demonstrate their genitals. Some men, mentally disturbed with a fixation on sex, expose their genitals to women passersby, while walking in the streets or traveling in the subway. The new eroticism contains all the symptoms typical of the nudity syndrome. In the play *Oh! Calcutta!* a young woman exhibits her genitals to the public, and perhaps finds sexual satisfaction in doing so.

The nudity syndrome is of particular interest from a psychological viewpoint. The basis of psychoanalysis is a nudification of the subconscious mind, particularly of all repressed sexual desires, according to Freud. A psychoanalyzed individual discloses all his hidden sex desires and gains freedom by "opening his subconscious mind" to the therapist. But such a psychological nudification of sex impulses and desires is of a purely psychological nature and this liberation of repressed sex impulses gives no real sexual gratification to the treated person. In the mind of a patient, sexual nudity is an essential part of complete freedom. A survey conducted by a group of medical men on psychoanalytical patients revealed that almost all of them, after or during therapy, experienced a compulsive desire to expose their sexual organs. This gave them not only a feeling of sexual freedom, but sometimes an illusory gratification often associated with obscenity. In fact, obscenity is an inseparable part of the nudity syndrome.

Obscenity is also an essential part of the new eroticism. For obscenity is declared by the avant-garde of certain intellectual groups as a symbol, an attribute of true freedom of sexual expression. An excellent illustration of this trend of our time is Philip Roth's novel, *Portnoy's Complaint*. A large part of this book is possibly pure imagination. It is essentially sensational, not in the facts that he describes but because of the use of filthy words. There is nothing new in this book which one cannot find in any popular medical book concerning sex and its abnormalities. From a strictly medical point of view, this novel is a fraud. It is, rather, a business enterprise, the way to produce a best seller—all because of its shocking obscenity. The striking thing is not so much the book itself as the warm and enthusiastic reception it received from our intellectuals and the public at large.

Dr. Ernest Van der Haag, professor of social philosophy at New York University mildly criticized the new wave of eroticism.[11]

"Freud described a process that is called repression in individuals: that which takes place when the individual is confronted with impulses that part of his personality has to reject —at least temporarily—because of fear of being swamped by these impulses. One way to look at censorship is to consider whether it may not be the social analogue of deeper repressions that take place in the individuals. That is, the society also, rightly or wrongly, finds it necessary to repress those things that it fears may swamp its order and impair its function. One danger in having pornography is in time it may come to resem-

---

[11]Quoted from the article by Jill Krementz, *Time*, July 11, 1969.

ble sex instruction in school: it can make sex as boring as it already is in Sweden and Denmark."

But Kenneth Tynan, organizer of *Oh! Calcutta!*, firmly defends the new eroticism and explains its significance for the liberation of sex:[12]

"Pornography seems to me a necessary and useful thing to have around as an adjunct to ordinary sex, and as an alternative to ordinary sex. I think it's a boon to the tired traveler—in a foreign country where he doesn't speak the language or doesn't know anybody. I think it's an absolute social necessity in the case of some people who are ugly and old and lonely, but that does not mean it should only be for the ugly, the old, and the lonely."

Dr. Van der Haag replied to Mr. Tynan, stressing the detrimental effect of depravity on true art.[13]

"Mr. Tynan's idea is apparently that pornography can be good, depending, of course, on the quality of who creates it. Now as I think of art it is not the experience itself, but a reflection upon experience. As Santayana put it, high art cancels lust. My view would be this: the better the writer, the less effective his writing as 'pornography' as you defined it, however sexual his subject may be."

While the discussion about the merit of the new eroticism is going on among authors and playwrights, pornography and obscene literature are spreading widely in this country. Men and women of upper and middle class wait for hours in long lines to see movies such as *I am Curious (Yellow)* and others in New York City and other towns of America just because they are obscene. The greatest danger is that obscene movies and books are reaching children.

[12] *Ibid.*
[13] *Ibid.*

One of many cases of the effect of pornography on youth was reported from Portland, Oregon. Mayor Terry Schrunk has a committee which tries to keep pornographic literature out of childrens' hands by encouraging local stores to ban it voluntarily from their sales racks. Recently one committee member got a phone call from a mother who had found her fourteen-year-old daughter in bed with a girl friend experimenting with lesbian practices which they were checking out in a manual on Sapphic love.

"It's virtually impossible to keep children from seeing the explicit movies and reading the pornographic literature," says Donald Sterling, Jr., editorial page editor of the Oregon *Journal.* "I can see very little hope for legislation to regulate it," he adds. "The prosecuting attorney told me he can't think of any obscenity law that he can enforce."

In Mitchell, S. D., 18-year-old Jeff Logan had been managing the family's Roxy Theater for two years and doing well in high school when local authorities seized the Roxy's print of *Candy* and charged him with obscenity. The prairie town of 14,000 promptly split into pro- and anti-*Candy* groups. From his pulpit, Dr. Swayne F. Knight, a Methodist minister, backed the seizure, which provoked a group of students from Mitchell's Dakota Wesleyan University into a protest walkout.

In the meantime, the Supreme Court has ruled that a man possessing pornographic films cannot be arrested and convicted as long as it was not proved that he was showing them outside of his home.

Individual analytic sessions with patients have greatly declined during the last few years. There are two fundamental reasons for neurotic patients' disappointment with this type of psychotherapy. First, it is often ineffective and if there is an improvement, it is of a temporary and subjective nature. Second, and no less important, whether a psychiatrist or a psycho-analyst is treating a neurotic, it is always a very expensive proposition. The patient is required to visit his doctor once or twice a week, for weeks and months, and in some instances for years. Patients are charged from $20 to $50 for a 50-minute session. Thus by the end of the therapy the patient will have paid $25,000 to $35,000 to his doctor.

Facing the possibility of losing their lucrative practice, the Freudian fellows concentrated their efforts on the mass confession technique. In almost no time they developed an enormously profitable business along these lines, organizing and guiding the so-called T-groups (also called sensitivity sessions or sensitivity groups). Jane Howard[14] described the various organizations in this country which practice mass confession, associated with induced increased sexuality through men and women touching each other. In some of these organizations the patients, or curious persons, are in early middle age, with teen-agers excluded from the sessions. The meetings take place during weekends, and the cost per person is $45 to $75. In most of the groups, sexual intercourse is forbidden, but in some of them the confession sessions require the participants to be nude, and to touch each other in the most sexual manner. The groups of men and women meet in the swimming pool, all nude, or on the lawn, and touch one another without speaking. The T-groups in the West are more liberal in regard to sexuality, while the Eastern groups are trying to be more conventional.

According to Miss Howard, the T-group movement is growing fast, attracting mostly middle-class persons. It seems that they are seeking not so much relief from their conflicts as

[14]Jane Howard, *Please Touch: A Guide of the Human Potential Movement*, New York: McGraw-Hill Book Company, 1970.

excitement of a sexual nature, brought about by the "touch-me" technique.

There are situations when a comment or summary is not essential, when the facts speak for themselves. That is the case of the tragic epidemic of exaggerated sexuality interwoven with pornography and obscenity in this country. This sexual epidemic was bred and fermented by the extreme permissiveness of our society, promoted and defended by our intellectual circles, contaminated by the Freudian concept of sexual freedom. It is in the field of sexuality that the influence of the permissiveness syndrome has reached its height.

9
•

Revolution or Permissiveness?

• •

BAKUNIN, the famous Russian leftist revolutionary of the
19th century, repeatedly said: "Only a man of high morality,
honesty, and integrity has the right to be a true revolutionary."
One should approach the so-called revolutionary movement in
this country from this viewpoint. For thousands of years there
have been revolutions in countless countries and nations, but
the "revolution in the U.S.A." differs from all the revolutions
of the past. There have been revolutions against tyranny, des-
potic governments, democracy, or political revolutions, where
two or more parties were fighting for power. But in all the cases
of revolution, there was not a single instance when it was directed against the country itself, the country to which the revolutionaries belonged and of which they were citizens.

And that is the extraordinary case, the exceptional case, of the present-day "revolutionary movement" in America.

On April 16, 1969, seven youths tore down and trampled an American flag during a well-photographed demonstration, and were arrested by FBI agents on charges of desecrating the flag.

U.S. Attorney William Meadows said the seven were charged with "casting contempt upon the flag by publicly defiling it." He said the seven were the first charged in his jurisdiction with violating a flag desecration law passed by Congress in 1968.

This was not the only case of trampling or burning the American flag. Destroying the national flag symbolizes the nature of the militant movement in this country. The flag does not represent the government, or capitalism, or industry, or the police, or any political party. It represents our country itself. Burning the flag demonstrates the hatred of our country by the militant youth, both white and black. The fact that in many demonstrations militants wave the flags of North Vietnam and the Vietcong only underlines the depth of their hatred for our nation. This does not prove their revolutionary spirit but only their dislike and rejection of everything that is America.

Most surprising is the attitude of the Supreme Court toward the desecration of the national flag and the insult to our country by militant youths.

The Supreme Court did not help the cause of law and order in America when they reversed a decision of the lower courts which had convicted a man of burning the American flag. In this instance, "freedom of speech" was given a much wider latitude than ever before.

In this flag-burning case, five justices voted to reverse the conviction, and four dissented. The defendant had been convicted of violating a law of New York state which makes it an offense to "mutilate, deface, defile, or defy, trample upon or cast contempt upon either by words or act" the American flag.

All the states of the Union and the District of Columbia have such laws. But the high court declared that the flag-burning was just an expression of protest.

Testimony was given that the defendant had cried out: "We don't need no damn flag," and that, when asked whether he had burned the flag, he had said: "Yes; that is my flag; I burned it." Yet the majority of the court concluded that this "amounted only to somewhat excited public advocacy of the idea that the United States should abandon, at least temporarily, one of its national symbols."

Mayo Mohs[1] gave an excellent illustration of militant youth's hatred for America, while he observed the behavior of demonstrators during the New York Moratorium March:

"Almost at once I could sense that these marchers were different. There was a fresh new hate in them, a bitterness hurled indiscriminately at the world around them. One girl—she could not have been more than 15—was taking particular delight in shrieking the obscene adjective loudly at the cop. The word was hardly new, but her strangely misdirected rage was. It was surely not *his* war.

"The Viet Cong flag passed, and I knew what the kids must have been told.

"Then came a Cuban flag, bold and bright, for a moment reminding me that once, when Castro was still in the hills, he looked like a hero to many of us. Then I remembered '*Al paredon* [To the Wall]!' and the betrayals that came before the sugar cane.

"I watched four blocks of the parade pass. Panther flags. Shouts of 'Off the pigs!' The Youth Against War and Fascism

---

[1]Mayo Mohs, "End of the March," *Time*, April 27, 1970.

under a red banner emblazoned with Lenin's portrait. Maybe they had not heard of the early, ugly Party tyranny that broke the heart of Lenin's romantic young American follower, John Reed. Behind them came another, newer cause, something more to cloud the main issue: 'Abolish all abortion laws.'

"Across the street they were there, ramming their way into the mad jumble of Bryant Park. Later, the militants—the YAWFs, the Progressive Labor SDS wing and others—fought their way onto the platform and kept off speakers they did not approve of. If that was the future, it, too, would be a joyless prize.

"What had we come to march against? The war? Which war? And against whom?"

Who are the radical militants who hate their country? The poor, the hungry, the deprived? Not at all. Most militant young boys and girls belong to well-to-do and upper-middle-class families. They have had everything in their lives. Some, spoiled by their parents from their childhood, were educated in expensive preparatory schools and are students at the elite Ivy League universities. And all of them are saturated with hate for the country which gave them more than they ever earned. Are they revolutionaries, as they call themselves in their ignorance, or are they products of extreme permissiveness of their parents and our society? They have no goal in their so-called revolutionary drive, except one: to destroy everything that they can put their hands on. Many of them use drugs, are involved in excessive sexual activity, and infected with venereal diseases. Bakunin would reject their claim to being revolutionaries. These sons and daughters of wealthy indulgent parents are bored. In their wild acts they search for excitement and gratification in an attempt to fill their spiritual emptiness.

And what is the reaction of the American liberals? They call these displaced youths "revolutionaries" as emphatically as Associate Justice William O. Douglas[2] did when he claimed: "The present student riots are similar to the revolution for American independence . . . for we must realize that today's Establishment is the new George III." And he ends his small pamphlet with a warning: "If the Establishment resolves to suppress the dissenters, America will face, I fear, an awful ordeal."[3]

To the American liberals there is little if any doubt that this country is confronted with a true revolution. There is an element of excitement and pleasure in this idea, which is often reflected in newspaper and TV commentaries on the events which have been taking place in this country during the last few years. Yet many scientists find that extreme permissiveness is the cause, or one of the causes of riots.

Dr. Bruno Bettelheim,[4] director of the Sonia Shankman School for psychotic children at the University of Chicago writes: "American parents and American society have not given today's youth the emotional equipment for engaging in rational and constructive protest."

In part he blames the permissiveness of parents, their "half-baked psychoanalytic" ideas, the national insistence on putting high school graduates indiscriminately into the isolated academic atmosphere of traditional colleges and universities, and other reasons.

All of which draws some support and some dissent from a Tampa psychiatrist and a sociologist at the University of South Florida.

"Young people want a structure and they are mad because no one has given them that," said Dr. Jerry Fleischaker, psychiatrist and director of the Hillsborough County Guidance Center.

[2]William O. Douglas, *Points of Rebellion,* New York: Vintage Press, 1970, p. 95.
[3]*Ibid.*, p. 97.
[4]*Encounter*, November 1969, London, England.

"He [Bettelheim] implies that a lot of student radicals are somehow mentally ill . . . disturbed from youth . . . that is not really fair," said Dr. Don Schneller, professor of sociology at the University of South Florida. But he agrees that youths need discipline.

Bettelheim, who sees some student radicals in his private therapeutic practice and observes others on the University of Chicago campus, goes further:

"The political content of student revolt is most of all a desperate wish that the parent should have been strong in the convictions that motivate his actions. This is why so many of our radical students embrace Maoism, why they chant 'Ho Ho Ho Chi Minh' in their demonstrations. They chant of strong fathers with strong convictions."

Dr. John William Ward, professor at Amherst College said that Americans are taught to believe that they are free to make of their lives what they can, with nothing to encumber their progress but themselves.

When that ideal meets the reality of failure for some, "there is no place to turn rage and frustration except inward against one's self, and no way to understand it except as an irrational and aberrant pattern of behavior.

"The American ideology of personal freedom leads to a massive frustration which easily spills over into violent behavior when the reality of the social situation, the lived experience of people, blocks and prevents them from acting out what they are told is ideally possible."[5]

One may add to what Dr. Ward said, that when an emotionally and intellectually immature boy or girl is convinced that he has the right of unlimited freedom, as the majority of youth now have, it is the embodiment of permissiveness.

[5]84th Annual Meeting of the American Historical Association, Washington, D.C.

Not all Americans believe, as does Supreme Court Associate Justice Douglas, that there is a revolution in this country. Tom R. Shepard, Jr., publisher of *Look* magazine, discusses this matter in his magazine: "The young people of America—and I refer now to the overwhelming majority of boys and girls, not to the tiny SDS minority—do not provoke, support, or endorse the revolutionary movement.

"Let me offer some evidence. Not long ago, a *Look* colleague of mine attended an alumni dinner at Rutgers. He tells me he went to that dinner with some trepidation. He expected to be surrounded by a mob of unwashed and unkempt young men and pelted with obscene remarks about the Establishment, if not with cutlery. Why did he expect this reception? Because he, like most of us, had been brainwashed into believing that this was the appearance and attitude of American youth. Well, according to my friend, from the moment he stepped into the dining room until the moment he left, it was one surprise after another. First off, every one of the two thousand students was wearing a necktie and a jacket. And what did these college seniors talk about? Were they plotting a campus riot? A march on Washington? Did they attack the Establishment? Not in the least. What they wanted to know—are you listening out there, you prophets of revolution?—was what kind of pension system we had at *Look* magazine. And what salaries could they expect to get if they went to work in our—get this—Sales Department?"[6]

It is well known that many clergymen are contaminated by Freudian ideas about sex and guilt and permissiveness.

Here is the remarkable suggestion of Dr. Roger Johnson, who is in charge of clinical pastoral education for the Lutheran Hospital Society, Los Angeles, California:

[6]Lakeland (Florida) *Ledger, March 14, 1970.*

"Perhaps the more we promote intimacy, the less manifestations of violence we should have." Dr. Johnson cites the openness toward sex of the homogenous Scandinavian countries, their generally peaceful societies, and their virtual limitation of the term "obscene" to physical violence.

Violence, and the tendency toward aggression, he stated, was an inherited trait of man.

"But in sexuality, the growth of intimacy, there may be a possible way of channeling and redirecting these impulses."

It is certainly an original approach to riots and revolution, but one should remember that the majority of youth involved in riots are already deep in sexuality and narcotics. And crimes of violence are very high both in Sweden and Holland.

Vandalism in Elementary and Secondary Schools

A striking event occurred near New York City. Vandals systematically damaged calculators and laboratory equipment, flooded the building with fire hoses, overturned furniture, and splashed paint all over the walls. Something like that happens every week in some community, but this example was notable because it occurred in one of the wealthiest and most stable suburban communities in the U.S.: Greenwich, Connecticut. There, in a city that has no serious racial or community problems, the intruders damaged the high school to the extent of more than $10,000 and forced it to close down for a day.

The sabotage in Greenwich will be added to a national bill that has already reached staggering proportions—and it is rising steeply every year. No one can fix an accurate price tag on vandalism, which is not always reported, not always identifiable as such, and covers everything from toilet graffiti to arson. The U.S. Office of Education in Washington sets the annual cost of destruction in public schools at more than $100 million. In New York City, the cost of school vandalism amounted to an estimated $6.5 million last year. Why, in an era of unprecedented prosperity, has an increase in the most senseless of all crimes taken place against property?

What are the factors or causes of this epidemic of vandalism? Dr. Philip G. Zimbardo, a psychologist at Stanford University, and a leading U.S. authority on the anatomy of vandalism, after years of study and experimentation, has come up with his own theory of the national surge in such destruction. The vandal is typically young and the young of today care little for the society their fathers built. Furthermore, in an age of expanding permissiveness, the vandal is no longer so heavily concentrated, if he ever was, among the underprivileged and the poor. As sociologist Martin has noted, vandalism cannot be classified along racial, ethnic, or even economic lines.

Contemporary life invites the vandalistic act. The media play so endlessly on themes of violence and aggression they they become, to the young at least, an accepted part of life. Wholesale renunication of traditional values—the death of faith, the obsolesence of marriage, the campus as a locale for riots, the cop seen as pig—casts the adolescent adrift from all moorings.[7]

And here again we are returning to extreme permissiveness as the obvious cause of vandalism.

An Associated Press survey shows that malicious destruction —ranging from arson to window breaking—increased in several major cities between 1967 and 1968, sometimes by 25 or 30 percent. Estimates for the 1970–1971 school year indicate still more increases.

The cost of vandalism in the nation's school systems is increasing sharply, with total annual losses now estimated up to $200 million.

Window breakage alone in New York City cost $1.2 million

[7] *Time*, January 19, 1970, p. 45.

in 1970—$200,000 more than in 1967 and almost one fourth of the city's estimated $5 million total loss to vandalism in 1968.

In Philadelphia, the nation's fourth largest city, losses from "schoolboy mischief" were set at $1 million, up from an estimated $750,000 in 1967. Washington, D.C., estimated $400,-000 in losses last year, up from $250,000. Milwaukee estimated $335,000, up from $214,000.

Vandals in Atlanta filled plumbing drains with gravel, spread tar over freshly painted walls, and damaged air-conditioning equipment.

In Philadelphia three children did $20,000 damage in one afternoon—tore out plumbing, ruined television sets, ripped telephones from the walls, tore files apart, and upset desks and chairs.

In Baltimore, arsonists caused $1.5 million damage in 1968. Already there have been 10 fires in 1969, including the total loss of two schools, $450,000 and $600,000.

As an experiment, an intercom system was left on overnight in one school in Phoenix, Arizona. Sounds of a break-in would be heard by private police in another part of town, aiding in faster notification of watchmen. School officials said knowledge of the system apparently has reduced vandalism at that school.

In Kansas City, Missouri, where $408,000 in damages was reported last year, burglar alarms were installed and dogs patrolled school buildings.

Most officials figure vandalism is done by children who hit a school on the spur of the moment. But there are other instances of gangs breaking into schools and destroying them.

Lawrence L. Knutson of the Associated Press[8] reported that the nation's public schools are becoming fortresses. A national survey indicates that some of the largest school systems have

[8]Tampa [Florida] *Tribune*, March 5, 1970.

turned to barbed wire, floodlights, police dogs, heavy iron grilles, plastic windows, and an array of alarms and electronic surveillance systems, to reduce the cost of vandalism.

A survey conducted last year by the Baltimore public school system and released by a U.S. Senate juvenile delinquency subcommittee, said that 36 school systems, answering a questionnaire, reported a $6.5 million in vandalism and arson loss in the 1967–68 school year.

"The Baltimore study reads like something out of a World War II movie," a Senate aide said. "It is one of the firmest indications we have had that the problems of school vandalism and violence are getting out of hand."

Orlando F. Furno, an assistant Baltimore school superintendent and head of his system's research admitted: "There's no panacea, I can tell you that. The problem is simply too widespread and too complex."

Paul Harvey[9] describes anarchy in the Chicago schools. Today, Chicago's schools are torn by violence and threatened with anarchy. A spokesman for the teachers' union says that more than 700 Chicago area teachers go daily to their classes in fear for their personal safety.

"Gangs which fight, assault, intimidate may be dealt with by expulsion. But when you discipline a gang member, his gang may retaliate in a manner which compounds the problem.

"The undisciplined and frequently violent student is, of course, not peculiar to Chicago. In other cities, teachers reportedly carry guns to school for self-defense.

"But Chicago, which once boasted a 'model school system,' has suffered perhaps the severest setback.

"Total assaults on teachers have increased from 135 in 1964 to 854 in 1969.

[9] Lakeland (Florida) *Ledger*, May 6, 1970.

"There is not yet available a 1969 tally of instances of homocide, forcible rape, robbery, aggravated assault, burglary, vandalism, weapons offenses, drunkenness, drug law violations, or other offenses committed by students."

Apparently only a small minority of school pupils are vandals. The vandals react more than the majority of pupils to the atmosphere of permissiveness. They—the vandals—are rarely punished, and if there is a penalty, it is insignificant. One may ask the logical (or illogical) question: Are these young school vandals revolutionaries?

I asked a number of schoolteachers and college faculty members this question. Among them were conservatives, liberals, and two radicals. Except for one radical, an instructor of sociology at a local college, all the others rejected flatly the idea that the vandalism in public schools was a revolutionary movement and that the children were revolutionaries. The radical, as he called himself, was inclined to believe that school vandalism was a reflection of the revolutionary movement in this country.

But when I asked the same persons: "Is the vandalism at college and university campuses a manifestation of a revolutionary movement and are the college vandals revolutionaries?" except for the two conservative professors, the group was inclined to consider the campus vandals as revolutionaries.

Vandalism on American College Campuses

During the last four years, vandalism on U.S. college campuses has cost millions of dollars. No exact figures are available, but the cost of campus vandalism was many times higher than that in public schools. Half of the colleges from California to the East Coast were ransacked. From San Francisco State College and Berkeley to Columbia, Yale, and Harvard, to the University of Utica—all were assaulted by student vandals, leaving the institutions with broken windows, smashed doors, destroyed valuable manuscripts and files, broken typewriters and priceless apparatus, burned valuable paintings and records. Both whites and blacks took part in this irresponsible rampage. The vandals almost always invaded the offices of the president and admission officers as if, in their naive concept, it gave them the illusion of exerting power over their university.

The behavior of American student vandals has proved their immaturity, has demonstrated that they did not deserve to be associated with institutions of higher education.

Campus Riots in America

Many leading politicians, such as Eugene McCarthy and Edward Kennedy, proclaimed that campus riots are a "revolution." While the liberals adhere to this position, the large majority is inclined to believe that this campus movement is a manifestation of permissiveness on the part of the college administrations and passivity on the part of the majority of students. The problem is complex and deserves to be analyzed objectively. The chief question is whether the campus riot is a revolutionary movement or the result of the permissiveness which prevails in this country.

One of the most impressive examples was the riot at Cornell University. Rowland Evans and Robert Novak[10] reported on the situation at Cornell University after an armed invasion of its administrative offices by a group of militant students. Even before the student invasion took place, "Militant black students were showing up for classes they had not registered in, taking seats in the rear, and carefully jotting down the professor's words. The message to the faculty members: Any remark that might in the slightest way offend Negro sensibilities could only invite trouble.

[10]Tampa [Florida] *Tribune*, April 22, 1969.

"Furthermore, such intrusions on academic freedom have been tolerated by President James A. Perkins. In an interview here, Perkins described to us a conflict between 'social justice' and 'academic freedom,' adding that he was 'a mugwump' straddling the two positions. However, Perkins continued, he had told faculty members they 'could not use the cloak of academic freedom' to cover up statements which might anger black students.

"Thus, when the Perkins administration capitulated to black demands at gunpoint, the minority of professors dedicated to academic freedom—most of them in the government and history departments—determined they had no place in Cornell's new order. They reasoned that the black militants always could force the administration to surrender when classroom content was at issue.

"Even more disturbing to them is the feeling that Cornell is no isolated catastrophe. The professors fleeing from here are haunted by the fear that the tradition of academic freedom may be dying in America and that Cornell is but the outrider of that calamity.

"Certainly, Cornell is about to undergo drastic change. The professors who have resigned or are likely to resign are among the university's most respected scholars and teachers (such as government Professor Walter Berns, winner of this year's teaching award). Those students on both graduate and undergraduate levels who are attracted here by such teachers are seeking to transfer for the next term. Moreover, with the notoriety it has now achieved, Cornell will henceforth be vastly more attractive to the student agitator than to the serious student.

"Nor does this seem repugnant to either the administration or a majority of the faculty. Perkins is actively supporting the self-proclaimed 'constitutional convention' of faculty and students which began meeting in Barton Hall after the bloodless black insurrection. This effort to 'restructure' the university is aimed at a new order where students help decide what is taught and how it is taught."

Twenty-four hours later, the faculty Council of Cornell University recommended that the school give in to militant Afro-American students on a disciplinary case and called a faculty meeting to reconsider the issue.

The action came only one hour after a spokesman for the student group warned on the campus radio station that the university "has three hours to live" unless penalties in the case were nullified.

A university spokesman said the council decision was made earlier in the day before Thomas R. Jones, a member of the Afro-American students, taped a statement giving the university an ultimatum to act by 9 P.M.

"We are going to demonstrate . . . we may die . . . we may die but we're not going to die alone," Jones said. On Monday night, the full faculty of this university of 14,000 students had refused to meet key demands of the Afro-Americans. Instead they condemned black student actions. Following that action, Faculty Dean Robert B. Miller announced he had resigned as an "act of faith" with the students.

Miller said he had put his job "on the line" in negotiations Sunday to end the armed occuption of Willard Straight Hall.

The faculty council's action amounted to complete capitulation to the militant group of Cornell Negroes who took over a campus building Saturday and emerged with guns Sunday.

On Sunday, June 1, 1969, Cornell University president James A. Perkins, target of intense criticism for his handling of campus racial incidents, announced his intention to resign.

Dr. Perkins' announcement came on the heels of the resignation of the presidents of City University of New York and Washington's Federal City College.

Dr. Perkins told the Cornell *Daily Sun* he had received letters and telegrams running "five to one" against him.

The invasion of militant students and their seizure of the administrative buildings does not always end peacefully.

The president of Swarthmore College died of a heart attack in his office while Negro students held control of the college admissions office for the eighth day.[11]

The Quaker-affiliated school near Philadelphia was thrown into near shock by the death of Dr. Smith. Colleagues said he had been under "a strain" since about 25 blacks took over the admissions office to enforce demands for more Negro students, faculty, and administrators, and a role in policy making.

Dr. Courtney Smith, 52, Swarthmore president, succumbed shortly before he was to meet with a faculty committee which had been studying demands made by Negro demonstrators.

The most extraordinary events took place in a California college. For almost three years, San Francisco State College was the arena for violent riots, with arson, bombing, breaking of furniture and valuable instruments, assaulting of professors, and sit-ins which forced the closing of the college several times. The college was an illustration of how apparently uncontrollable campus riots have become, specifically when the Students for a Democratic Society (SDS) directs the riots.

And then Dr. Samuel Ichiye Hayakawa, Japanese-American, world-renowned semanticist, was named acting president. In six months the college began to function almost normally. There were no more riots, nor arson, nor strikes. His guide to meet student violence or other disturbances was a quotation from the British pacifist, Bertrand Russell: "The only excuse for

THE PERMISSIVE SOCIETY

the use of force is to reduce the total amount of force in the world."

It was working. It was getting results. There is little overt violence, and students and faculty know Dr. Hayakawa will not tolerate it.

In his brilliant article,[12] Dr. Hayakawa reveals his ideas and opinions about campus riots:

> "All over the country people have been sorely puzzled by the violent rebellion of young men and women in our best colleges and universities—Berkeley, Harvard, Columbia, Swarthmore, Stanford—I hesitate to mention San Francisco State in the context of these more prestigious institutions.
>
> "Many of the general public are infuriated that the most highly privileged young should be the least grateful for their privileges.
>
> "I too have been sorely puzzled. But I want to submit a possible explanation. Perhaps we are having these troubles not because our colleges have failed us, but because they have in some ways done their work too well.
>
> "Most student rebels are of the upper-middle class. They are to be found largely in the liberal arts departments and the social sciences—disciplines in which verbal facility is highly prized, and in which it is not always necessary to check one's words against the stubborn facts of life (as you have to in chemistry or home economics) in order to pull down an 'A.'
>
> "The cards are stacked in favor of the verbalists. Tests of scholastic aptitude are easy for those with a ready flow of words.
>
> "Those who do well in such tests are courted, sometimes by two or more prestigious colleges. They can hardly be blamed if they begin to feel superior. From there on they can succeed in college without really trying. All they have to do is major in English or Sociology.
>
> "Furthermore, the liberal arts student is heir to a tradition that goes back to the ancient Greeks of distinguishing between the 'liberal' and 'servile' arts.
>
> "The liberal arts curriculum was for the education of gentlemen, who by definition did not work for a living.
>
> "The 'servile' arts—from cooking to barbering to commerce to engineering—were for workers and slaves.

---

[12]The *Register* and *Tribune* Syndicate.

"The ancient Greek prejudice against work is reflected to this day in the American university in the scorn of many liberal arts professors of 'vocationalism' and in the contempt of many English majors for such subjects as commerce, engineering, agriculture and chemistry.

"Laden with such prejudices, the verbalists find it easy to define themselves as an intellectual aristocracy—an elite class—and to begin to act like one.

"As an elite, these white students believe themselves to be above the conventions and restraints of everyday life.

"They despise the useful citizen and take pleasure in shocking the lower and middle classes by outrageous speech, dress, and behavior.

"They will not be bothered discussing or arguing matters with those with whom they disagree—they simply want their own way at once, by force if necessary.

"Let me add that the nonviolent majority also identifies with the underdog. The present student generation is seriously concerned with society. It is this seriousness that makes them susceptible to revolutionary propaganda, with the result that many young people who genuinely believe in democracy are sometimes led around by those who do not.

"Many professors are elitists too, indoctrinating students in the rejection of middle-class standards and encouraging resistence to administration, government, and police.

"Radical pressure groups dominating faculty meetings blocked the introduction both of resolutions condemning student violence and of resolutions calling for police protection against that violence, presumably feeling that the elite ought to settle things among themselves without the intervention of the lower classes.

"Can professors, luxuriating in their academic freedom, stop short of an egotistic irresponsibility that threatens the very existence of the academy?

"And can young people of outstanding talents be given a superior education without their ending up believing that they are a superior order of being, immune to control by custom or law, exempt from the responsibilities of rational discourse and debate, possessed of the right to dictate to others through nonnegotiable demands, and entitled to amnesty the moment they get into trouble?"

Dr. Hayakawa gave a clear picture of the causes responsible for campus riots.

A leading role in American campus riots is played by the student organization called the Students for a Democratic Society, mentioned earlier. This organization originated in Ivy League universities. The name of the organization is misleading. The SDS does not fight for the preservation of democracy. Members are definitely anti-democratic. They advocate the principle that a small minority has the right to dictate to a large majority. In fact they behave in a fascistlike manner. They believe that they have the right to use any means to achieve their goal, and their goal is to destroy The Establishment. Yet they offer nothing with which to replace it.

Who are the members of this organization? As Dr. Hayakawa stressed, many of them belong to the upper class who are or were students at elite Ivy League universities. Some of them are brilliant students with a pathological arrogance. They are bored and, to some extent, their present "revolutionary" activity is to escape from boredom. They play at "revolution," and this brings them publicity from the media and admiration from the student masses. But most of all it brings them excitement. They have exhausted sex and dope. They do not hesitate to use arson and bombing, burning buildings to stimulate their tired nerves. The records of their destructive activity are hardly honorable.

"It finally happened to Harvard. . . ."[13] The conflict began at noon. About 250 students from Harvard and Radcliffe, most of them members of SDS, appeared outside University Hall, the three-story administration building at the center of Harvard Yard. They reiterated six "unnegotiable" demands made on the Harvard Corporation. The issues: the abolition of ROTC and

[13] *Time*, April 18, 1968.

an end to what the radicals consider Harvard's "expansionist" approach to its urban surroundings.

Chanting "Fight! Fight!" the students marched into the hall, which contains the offices of the Harvard deans, though not the university president's office. When one of the five deans asked the students to leave, he was jeered and shouted down. The rebels then forcibly evicted the deans and their assistants. They locked themselves inside the building, securing the doors with red bicycle chains, and proceeded to hold meetings to discuss further strategy. "The Corporation," their proclamation grandly noted, "can issue a statement when it gives in."

The SDS radicals and their allies had clearly violated Harvard's tradition of open communication and rational discourse.

Harvard President Nathan Pusey, after consulting with the trustees and faculty members, called the police. Shortly before dawn 400 policemen entered the Yard. About half were state troopers; the rest were drawn from the constabularies of Cambridge, Boston, and other parts of the metropolitan area. Facing them on the south steps of University Hall were about 120 students, with wet pieces of torn bedsheets to put on their faces in case tear gas was used. Dean Fred L. Glimp of Harvard College gave the radicals one last chance. "You have five minutes to vacate the building," he announced over a bullhorn, but his words were drowned out by students chanting in unison: "Pusey must go; ROTC must go!"

The troopers charged. In less than a minute the students were pushed and shoved, punched and clubbed, and driven from the steps. Then, after unlimbering sledgehammers, chain cutters, and a four-foot iron battering ram, the troopers forced their way into the building. Screams of anger and pain were heard inside. The troopers began removing the protesters, dragging some away by their long hair and striking others with billy clubs. By 5:30 A.M., a mere 25 minutes after they made the initial charge, the police had cleared the building.

More recently, on April 15, 1970 there was a riot in Harvard Square. Laurence T. May, student at Harvard, described it:[14]

"I was there for a lot of the action and will agree with the newspaper statement. The mob was the most ugly I have ever seen. The ferocity, the determination, the hatred they felt for the police was frightening. People who think that these kids are only frustrated youth, upset about the war or whatever, have no conception of what they are really dealing with in situations like this riot. I don't think I'm at all astray if I say that what I witnessed was nothing more than the collective expression of the criminal mind.

"These students were, a lot of them anyway, on drugs. I have never seen groups of 'kids' quite as literally mad as I saw Wednesday. They were shrieking, chanting, yelling; the ones with painted faces added to the barbaric imitations." This riot was organized by the SDS.

Another near riot was provoked by the SDS at Princeton University. More than 75 Princeton University students occupied an administration building to protest the school's investments in companies doing business in South Africa.

In the afternoon, 40 white students left the building and 35 Negroes remained inside.

Shortly after 6:30 P.M. the rest of the students left the building after being served with summonses by the university's disciplinary committee, a university spokesman announced.

Dr. Robert F. Goheen, the university president, said the occupation of the building had interrupted the processing of

[14]Tampa *Tribune*, April 26, 1970.

applications for admission and halted the completion of the school's biweekly payroll.

There are 3,200 undergraduates at the 223-year-old Ivy League institution.[15]

Fires damaged two wings of a Stanford University building shortly after police broke up a student demonstration against the ROTC.

Authorities said fires in two separate wings of a Stanford University studies center were believed to have been set by arsonists. Damages were estimated at between $50,000 and $100,000.[16]

On April 13, 1970, student demonstrators used a steel pipe battering ram to break down the office door of Massachusetts Institute of Technology President Howard Johnson and occupied his office.

About 200 youths led by members of SDS of MIT gathered in the administration area lobby at noon and marched up to the second floor.

Six youths, wearing ski masks which hid their faces, wielded a makeshift battering ram made of steel pipes fastened together and fitted with handles. They knocked the door off its hinges and gained entrance to the private office of President Johnson, who was not in the building at the time.

About 50 youths remained to occupy his office, the adjoining reception room, and a dean's office on the other side of the reception rooms. Witnesses said the president's private files were opened and copy machines in the office were running.

[15]Associated Press, March 11, 1970.
[16]United Press International, April 25, 1970.

The military operation in Cambodia ordered by President Nixon provoked a new series of campus riots, starting with Kent State University, where students burned the ROTC building and attacked the National Guard. Four students were shot and killed.

This time, many university presidents and faculties took part in the protest against the Cambodian operation, according to Jeffrey D. Alderman.[17]

Yale University President Kingman Brewster, Jr., called for a nationwide effort by college students and teachers "to put pressure on the Nixon administration to end the war and to cease its attacks on the students and the universities."

Fires were reported at 11 campuses, with ROTC buildings as the main targets. Students on some campuses staged sit-ins in college buildings and blocked streets at others. National Guardsmen were on standby duty near several campuses.

The campus protests against Nixon's Indochina policies and the deaths of four students at Kent State University by Ohio National Guardsmen were mostly peaceful, however.

A student strike information center set up at Brandeis University reported student strikes at 319 schools. A similar organization at Antioch College said 348 campuses had strikes.

Many campuses in the country had no demonstrations and some individuals and organizations spoke out against the anti-war activity.

President S. I. Hayakawa of San Francisco State College said some of the students were being "led by anarchists."

The inside story of bloody riots at Kent State University was revealed by Victor Riesel.[18] The majority of students at Kent State University are from working class families due to the low cost of tuition.

[17]Associated Press, May 8, 1970.
[18]Tampa *Tribune*.

For some time Kent State University had been the target for the Ohio region SDS and the Akron communes.

"There was the looting, the burning, the attacks on banks, the assault on firefighters, and the destruction of inventories of small businessmen which hit Kent State University last week. Let's go back some years when the SDS's national self-appointed female revolutionist, Bernadine Dohrn, created herself in the image of a young Russian woman who, almost 100 years ago, became the sole survivor of a band of bomb-making terrorists who even then worked with electrical gadgets.

Bernadine, who sees herself as a latter-day La Passionaria, is one of several national SDS leaders. It is she who targeted Kent State University for quite a while. Then on April 28, 1969, she spoke to a student crowd in William Hall."

A week later, on May 6, almost exactly a year before the awesomely tragic shooting of four students, the SDS helped whip up a rally. Joyce Cecora, reportedly an important SDS speaker, bluntly called for the use of arms to end "the repressive action of the administration."

On February 27, 1969, Joyce Cecora had said that, unless the administration gave way, the SDS would burn and level the campus.

"Blood, now rotting the earth of Kent's lovely campus, did not spill accidentally. That soil was tilled—furrowed by the clanging iron words of the toughest band of nihilists this land has known. Virtually all of them are outsiders. Virtually all of them chose Kent State because it is what it is, a source of strength for American forces, a source of learning for the children of working people, a spot in middle America."

Going through the several hundred campus riots, and analyzing their cause and initiation, we see the same pattern. A small group of SDS, often less than 20, provoked or tried to provoke a confrontation between the administration of the college and the student body. As a rule they occupy the administration buildings or burn the ROTC.

How will the college president react? If he submits to their demands, usually related to the war, the SDS gains admiration and support of the student masses. It becomes popular. If, however, the college president takes a strong stand, this gives the SDS an opportunity to start larger riots.

And what is the role of Negro militants or Black Panthers in the college riots? Dr. Hayakawa explains that "collegiate rebels" (meaning SDS) are considering themselves the "aristocracy of the intellect" and are using Negro students as "cannon fodder."

". . . Blacks are recruited to be cannon fodder in a revolution planned by whites," Hayakawa said. "To use a phrase I detest, but which is in this instance all too descriptive, white revolutionaries by their largesse are making 'house niggers' of their black allies.

"And when the crackdown on revolutionary activities comes, it will be the blacks who will go to prison, not the whites."[19]

The strategy of the SDS is peculiarly the same in every campus riot. Nothing is left to the imagination. It is standardized. It works often, perhaps too often. The amazing aspect of this strategy is that the SDS duplicates tactics used by Benito Mussolini. At the time when he still was a member of the Italian Socialist party, Mussolini gave much attention to university revolts. He believed that the "power revolution," his type of revolution, should be initiated at the universities. He formed small nuclei of his followers at the universities and they became later the basis of the Fascist party.

Are the Students for a Democratic Society revolutionaries?

---

[19]Dr. Hayakawa's speech before a Senate subcommittee investigating campus violence, May 13, 1969.

This depends on what one considers a revolutionary to be. Webster's dictionary calls a revolutionary a person who wants radical changes. That is also what Mussolini and the fascists wanted. To form a better interpretation and understanding of this word, I must refer to my own revolutionary activity as a student in pre–Soviet Russia.

From my high school days, I was involved in the revolutionary movement. As a youngster of 16, I joined the Social Revolutionary party, and took an active part in it. The Social Revolutionary party was the creation of the Russian intelligentsia. The goal, the only goal of our party was democracy, as a political and spiritual concept.

I was arrested and spent several months in a cell in solitary confinement at the political prison known as Predvarilka. Much later I was elected a member of the All Russian Constituent Assembly and the Chairman of the Military Committee. Thus, being a part of it, I was in a good position to observe university student revolutionary activity.

Russian students participated in great numbers in the revolutionary movement directed against the monarchy. Many hundreds of them were killed during street demonstrations or in the barricades. Thousands were kept in jail or sent to Siberia. Many of them were executed. But while students were active outside the universities, there were never any riots inside of them. Revolutionary students never attempted to create riots by assaulting the university administration, or destroying the libraries or laboratories, or engaging in sit-ins. All of them—the left radicals, the anarchists, the socialists—respected their Alma Mater. Their university was sacred to them. They were willing to die or to suffer long imprisonment or hard labor in Siberia —but they rejected the idea of a campus riot. It is here that the great difference exists between a true student revolutionary and the Students for a Democratic Society. Perhaps the origin of this difference lies in the fact that the great majority of Russian university students were from a low-income class who considered it a privilege to belong to the student body of a university, and not, as Dr. Hayakawa stressed, the sons and daughters of wealthy families.

All in all, the SDS might be called "revolutionaries," but only in a narrow sense along with Mussolini's fascists. In the case of the fascists there was also arrogance, aristocracy of intellect, and the strong conviction that they were born to lead the masses of inferior intellect.

The relative success of campus riots incited by the SDS was made possible only because of the permissiveness of campus administrations and/or faculties and the passivity of moderate students. The riot in the Sorbonne, Paris was ended when drastic measures were applied by the government. Rioting Japanese students were similarly pacified when punitive measures were applied to them.

Realizing that the very existence of academic freedom was at stake and that nothing can be accomplished by permissiveness, many of Columbia University's leading scholars and teachers formed an organization of tenured faculty to fight campus violence they attribute to "the actions of a minuscule group of extremists."

In its first public statement, the Council of Tenured Faculty of Columbia University said that the small groups of radicals threaten the students as well as the faculty.

"The university must not be an enclave of illegality," said the organization. "Membership in the university does not confer a privilege to break the law, nor does the university have the obligation to protect those who do so."

The action of the tenured faculty came after episodes of window-breaking, disruptions of disciplinary hearings, sit-ins, bomb scares, and threats on the Columbia campus.[20]

Faculty members of many other universities are slowly reaching the same realization of the necessity to fight for academic freedom and sanctity of the university. As an example, the SDS were banned on Purdue University campus. Yet one must admit that there are more than a few young instructors in the colleges and universities who openly support and encourage the activity of the SDS.

Realizing that their fascistlike activity is repugnant not only to the majority of the American people but also to the great majority of college students and faculty members, the SDS decided to embark on terrorism against the American public.

"Revolutionaries" claim to have set bombs which wrecked three skyscraper offices of major corporations in Manhattan: The Socony-Mobil building, the IBM building, and the General Telephone and Electronics building. And in Louisiana the 34-story state capitol building was dynamited, causing $500,000 damage. The Bank of America was bombed and burned. These bombings were spectacular acts.

The FBI and police in the most troubled cities assert that it is impossible to say how many bombers are loose in the land. A reasonable guess is that the number is less than 1,000. The toll of dead and wounded from bomb attacks in the past two years is about 100. However, damage is estimated to run into many millions of dollars.

An investigation by the Associated Press focused on key radical strongholds where some of the most intensive bombings and other destructive violence occurred. This investigation showed:

[20]New York *Times* News Service.

—There is no proof of a large, national, centrally directed bombing conspiracy or of any foreign involvement in the bombings.

—Some groups, most notably the SDS Weathermen, have publicly announced their commitment to violent activism and are working in underground cells. One such cell apparently was involved in the accidental detonation of explosives that destroyed a luxurious New York town house. Three persons died in the blast.

—Although indictments and other evidence point to Black Panthers' and other Negro extremists' involvement in the bombing, the main thrust appears to come from young whites, mostly with middle-class or wealthier backgrounds.

—Bombings are on the increase, and both police and radical leaders say the tempo is being stepped up.

Terrorism never solved anything. It never succeeded. Sooner or later, as the frequency of bombing by irresponsible youth increases, there will be a violent reaction in this country against those who favored and who still applaud and promote permissiveness, and who are indirectly responsible for the violence that has developed.

The analysis of the strategy and behavior of the Students for a Democratic Society gives impressive proof that this movement is not an idealistic revolutionary one, but is a drive for power by an arrogant yet brilliant group of young men and women, many of whom are from the upper class in America. Their tactics follow closely those of Mussolini's followers in the days when he was still associated with the Italian socialist party. There is little question in the mind of anyone who has studied the ideology and rise of fascism that the SDS are fascist-oriented. They are actually what we might call the neo-fascist party of America.

10

•

American Liberalism and Permissiveness

• •

WHAT is a liberal?

In order to understand properly the meaning and the nature of liberalism, we must go back to its origin.

According to Havelock,[1] a liberal is not a man of strong moral or political convictions. And this does not seem to agree with the common meaning of this word. Yet as we will explain

[1]Eric A. Havelock, *The Liberal Temper in Greek Politics*, New Haven: Yale University Press, 1957. Havelock approaches classical political philosophy from the positivistic point of view. According to him, positivist study of society is "descriptive," being opposed to "judgmental evaluation" (pp. 120, 368). He accepts the distinction between primitive men or savages and civilized men (pp. 186–7). See also Auguste Comte, *Cours de Philosophie Positive*, Paris: Société Positive, 1894; and Leo Strauss, *Liberalism, Ancient and Modern*, New York: Basic Books, 1968.

further, Havelock's diagnosis would be acceptable to many Americans if only we would modify this meaning by saying that a liberal might be politically amoral under certain circumstances. Havelock also stresses that the liberal regards all political and moral convictions as "negotiable" because he is extremely tolerant.

According to our own opinion, the liberal is basically permissive. Originally a liberal was a man who behaved in a manner becoming a free man as distinguished from a "slave." The classic analysis indicates that *liberality* is a virtue concerned with the utilization of wealth and the tendency toward giving. In a classic sense, the liberal as formulated by Aristotle is a captive of his need to share his wealth. According to Aristotle, the liberal should be exclusively interested in the liberal sciences and arts, for they are choices worthy for their own sake. The liberal man on the highest level esteems most highly the mind and its excellence and is fully aware of the fact that man at his best is autonomous of any authority.

The word "liberal" has undergone successive changes since the early nineteenth century. Now "liberal" and "liberality" mean lack of restraint. As Havelock stated: "It is of course assumed that by any common sense definition of the word liberal as it is applied in politics Plato is not a liberal thinker." According to Havelock, modern liberalism puts a greater stress on liberty than authority; it regards authority as a derivative solely from society, and society as spontaneous or automatic rather than as established by man. It denies the existence of any fixed norms, since norms are responses to needs and change with needs. There is a historical process which is progressive without, however, tending toward an end or a peak (p. 123). Liberalism conceives of the historical process as a continuation of the evolutionary process. It is historical because it regards the human characteristics as acquired and not as given. Basically liberalism is optimistic; it is "a genuine humanism which is not *guilt-ridden.* It is democratic. It traces morality less to outstanding men than to groups. It is in full sympathy with technological society and an international commercial system. It is empirical and pragmatic."

Those are the characteristics of American liberalism as we saw them in the past, in the days of Woodrow Wilson, William English Walling, and others.

American liberalism today has changed. Deeply and gravely altered. A "liberal" of today is very different from the liberal of Woodrow Wilson's years. There was a certain stability of opinions and ideology in the liberals of that time. As an example, they were uncompromisingly anticommunist. They had no illusions about the dictatorial and antidemocratic nature of Leninism. The liberals of today are vaguely sympathetic toward international communism and are obsessed by the illusion that the communists are our friends. Even more so. Many liberals of prominence defend North Vietnam, applauding the antiwar demonstrators bearing the flag of the Asiatic communist despotism and personally taking part in these demonstrations. An influential U.S. Senator, a self-claimed liberal, even announced that the best solution to this armed conflict would be for Hanoi to dominate all of Indochina. By this appeasing attitude American liberals are betraying the basis of liberalism—democracy. According to Havelock, the compromising and even friendly attitude of American liberals toward Russian communism is a manifestation of extreme tolerance, and almost amoral (the "negotiable behavior").[2]

This antidemocratic behavior of American liberals was the first step on the pathway toward the decline of true American liberalism.

[2] *Ibid.,* p. 123.

Today the most essential element in liberalism is the absence, at least partially, of restraint, as Havelock stressed more than once.

Referring to what was said in the first part of this book about the origin of Freudian influence in this country, we must remind ourselves that the intellectuals, the great majority of whom are liberals, first succumbed to Freudian ethics.

And with the natural inbred trend to absence of restraint, American liberals accepted extreme permissiveness with enthusiasm. A thousand-page book could be written reporting the approval of extreme permissiveness on the part of American liberals. Without exaggeration, one may state that the liberals are responsible for the chaotic condition in which our country now finds itself. Their speeches, articles, and books all promote unlimited permissiveness.

The liberals of today refuse to realize and to admit to any degree the penetrating, demoralizing influence of Freudian ethics on them. As was shown in persons subjected to psychoanalysis, this influence is devastating. Man loses his individuality. His self-reliance is affected, and he often becomes spineless and easily disturbed by mass psychosis. His initiative and independence of reasoning are lost, and he is easily influenced by the opinions of other people.

In this book we have reported the situation in our permissive society step by step. We gave the figures on crime. We pointed out that during the last decade, when the liberals were in full swing in this country, about 200,000 women were forcibly raped. However, the most significant fact is that not a single liberal writer or reporter or TV commentator ever brought this terrible fact to the attention of the public. There has been a complete silence on the part of our liberals, as if no such atrocious assault on American womanhood existed. Yet the same liberal press and the sociologists and political scientists and social workers claimed again and again that poverty, and only poverty, is responsible for crime, although the figures clearly demonstrate that poverty is an insignificant factor in the enormous rise of crime in this country.

The leaders of liberalism forcefully defend the popular liberal slogan of "law and justice" (rather than "law and order"), meaning that poverty and only poverty is responsible for crime, including the forcible rape of women. The Supreme Court, essentially liberal in its rulings, often makes it impossible to fight crime in this country.

And, with more than 10 million youths smoking marijuana and many youths turning to hard narcotics, liberal leaders such as Dr. James Goddard condone the use of marijuana as "harmless as aspirin."

And then sex in America: The liberals are leading the campaign for freedom of sex. Some liberal publishers, we do not need to mention their names, are publishing obscene books and journals which are demoralizing our youth.

Consider the vandalism in secondary schools and riots on the campuses. Here more than in any other field, the liberal newspaper and TV reporters and commentators have inflicted the greatest damage on American youth, presenting events in a one-sided view favorable to dissenters and militants.

American liberalism of the past was a dignified, constructive, creative movement. Earlier liberals were not "guilt-ridden" as are the liberals of today. Today the feeling of guilt emanates strongly from everything they say or write. The influence of Freud on the liberals of our generation is strikingly evident.

Historically, liberalism has often deserted its basic principle and has become engulfed in excessive nonrestraint. When this happens, liberalism starts to decay due to internal weakness and amorality. That seems to be the case of American liberalism of today.

As Joseph Alsop said in his article "Is Liberalism Dying?":

"The chances are that American liberalism, the strongest force in U.S. politics for a great many decades, is now politically moribund, or at least is going into eclipse. Rebirth, or re-emergence, will no doubt occur eventually. But in the best Greek mythological fashion, American liberalism now seems likely to be eaten by its own children, the militants, both student and black.

"Almost no liberals, whether in politics or in the groves of academe, as yet appear to be aware of the fate that probably awaits them. Arthur Schlesinger, Jr. has been hooted for courageously defending freedom of speech and publication against that bogus old pantaloon of the white New Left, Herbert Marcuse. All white liberals have tearfully submitted to the kicks and insults of the black New Left.

"But to American liberals in the year 1969, neither facts nor experience seem to have much importance. For so long, so very long, they have been articulately authoritative, they have commanded an audience, they have had their friends and spokesmen in the seats of the mighty."

Here Mr. Alsop touches the basic weakness of liberalism. Once it loses its authority with its followers and is confronted with the loud voice of radicalism, liberalism is condemned to die. In fact this has happened with American liberalism of today. The power of liberalism depends on its intellectual superiority and morality. Once it tries to appease and to follow the paths of radicalism, once it accepts permissiveness and demogagy, liberalism loses its political significance. It is no longer a progressive, creative movement. American liberalism is not the only liberal tradition to be a victim of self-destruction (i.e., prewar German liberalism).

In spite of their decline, American intellectual–liberals remain faithful to their long-established attitude toward nonliberals. Their attitude to those who are politically neutral or conservative is that of an elite, of an aristocrat, toward an ignoramus, a slave. They refuse even to enter into a discussion of world problems with nonliberals. They reject conservative or neutral books and articles without even reading them. As Dr. Hayakawa said, this superiority complex of the intellectual liberals is explained by their liberal arts education. They are vocalists, men who learned the use of words and speech and who regard as simply a nobody everyone who is not trained in vocalistic exercises. The great majority of intellectual and quasi-intellectual liberals have received a liberal arts education. The sociologists, the professors of English, the social workers or lawyers go through life without ever learning about natural science and the laws which direct the development of the human race. Ignorant as they are in this respect, they manipulate words with perfection. And through their vocalistic experience they exert an enormous influence on the sociopolitical life of this country. Or rather they did exert such an influence until they were replaced by the radicals. And, incidentally, radicals and militants are vocalists too, though their voices are considerably louder than those of the liberals.

The personality of a modern American liberal is (or should be) of intense interest to any psychologist or psychiatrist. Intellectual as he is, man of reasoning as he should be, this type of liberal rejects all common sense or analytical reasoning and finds no other pathway for self-realization except to follow the call of the extreme left.

The liberal of today is dichotomic, psychologically speaking —whether he is a politician, or professor, or a government employee, or a newspaperman. He is against society and The Establishment and applauds vigorously any attack on it by leftist youth. But at the same time he—the liberal of today— is a part of The Establishment. His livelihood depends on the same Establishment. Thus he is affected by inner conflicts, often of an acute nature. He is full of feelings of guilt, and too often he is neurotic. He is proud of being liberal, of this trademark attached to him. But there is also a strong inferiority complex reaction in him. He is not sure of himself, because he has no deep and well-formed liberal ideology and convictions, as had the liberal of the past. He has no specific program to defend. He depends to a great extent on the general trend of what is considered liberal. All this perplexity and doubt brings him to a state of neurosis. He is selfish. That is a typical Freudian trait. He relates everything in this world, all sociopolitical events to himself. His personal failings and failures make him more radical, more opposed to society at large and to The Establishment. As a Freudian fellow, he is apt to blame society for his own mistakes.

When I meet liberal intellectuals, and I often do, I have a very strong nostalgic feeling. Many of them now resemble Chekhov's heroes in their appearance, with their long hair and beards, and even in their manner of speaking. Yet there is a considerable difference between the American liberal intellectuals of today and Uncle Vanya of the Russian intelligentsia. Not only do American liberals tend to be rather materialistic in their personal drives, but they also have a peculiar sympathy if not admiration for Soviet Russia, while the Russian intelligentsia, with their progressive liberal beliefs, were uncompromisingly anticommunist.

There has existed for many years a strange psychopolitical phenomenon in this country. It is not easy to understand the basis of it, unless we call on Freudian theory to help us. For decades—it started with Franklin Delano Roosevelt—liberals have had a touching sentiment for Soviet Russia. They were nursing—and they still are—the groundless illusion that Soviet communists are men of sincerity, that they are our friends and of no danger to our country. This fantastic illusion, contradicting all the evidence, was not shattered by all the events which have taken place in Soviet Russia. Every agreement the communists have signed with other countries, they have crudely violated and betrayed. The invasion of the small Baltic countries —Estonia, Latvia, and Lithuania—as well as Czechoslovakia and Hungary; their constant support of North Vietnam and North Korea and other Asiatic despotisms; their anti-Semitism, the repression of freedoms, their persecution of writers and artists, without mentioning the barbaric rule of Stalin—in spite of all this, many liberal intellectuals still admire Soviet Russia. How can this be explained? What is the intrinsic motivation in this psychological phenomenon? Obviously the doctrine of communism, particularly communist tactics, are not acceptable and are even revolting to every American liberal who believes in democratic ideas.

To understand the psychology of the American liberal intellectual, we must return to what Havelock said about the attitude of modern liberals toward international communism: They regard all political and moral convictions as "negotiable." A liberal is extremely tolerant and, we may add, very permissive by his nature and his personality. (Except toward strongly *anti*-communist nations, of course.)

This permissiveness is particularly accentuated when the liberal intellectual is confronted with the problem of communism as a menace to this country. Let us take as an example a leading liberal intellectual, Senator J. W. Fulbright, chairman of the Senate Foreign Relations Committee. His sympathetic attitude toward Hanoi is well known. He has used all his power to make the war with Hanoi difficult for our government. He was against security measures, against the ABM and MIRV. He expressed, more than once, the most naive belief that if we reduce our nuclear strategic forces and armed strength, the

Russian communists would be more disposed to be friendly with us, and less dangerous to democratic countries. Under his constant pressure upon our government, he has helped reduce our strategic power below that of Soviet Russia. The government was also obliged to cut defense spending by more than 20 percent, while the Russian communists have spent an increasing amount of money on strategic weapons. On one weapons system alone, the SS-9, the Soviets have spent $9 billion, more than our entire strategic budget. And when news reached Washington that Soviet Russia is building a submarine base in Cuba, Senator Fulbright immediately minimized the importance of this information. He said this "news" was designed to alarm the American people. "It happens every year at appropriations time," he told United Press International. "Last year, it was the SS-9 missiles. Now it's a submarine base. They are hoodwinking the American people and they are using the press to do it."[3]

When the news about the Cuban submarine port persisted, Senator Fulbright admitted that "the relative strength of the United States and Russia has changed since the Cuban missile crisis under President John F. Kennedy. It was possible at that time to bluff them, I think. I doubt that it is possible now because the best information we have is that there is a degree of parity. It is dangerous situation."

Fulbright did not mention that he was instrumental in transforming our country from the most powerful one to one less strong than Soviet Russia might be. Two weeks later, when it was confirmed that Soviet Russia had nearly completed a nuclear submarine base on the south coast of Cuba, in Cienfuegos[4] Senator Fulbright said nothing. He preferred to remain silent.

[3]Tampa *Tribune,* October 5, 1970.
[4]*Time,* December 21, 1970.

The tragic story of the permissive and appeasing attitude of liberal intellectuals toward Soviet Russia and international communism completes this book on the Freudian influence on American liberal intellectuals, the consequences of this contamination, and the unquestionable menace of this permissiveness to the health, the morale, and even the very existence of our country. Yet in spite of all the ills which were brought about by our permissive liberals, I believe that the natural strength of our nation will overcome all the difficulties and will gradually reduce considerably the influence of liberal intellectuals, and will free this country from Freudian ethics.

As a biologist, believing in the future of the human race developing along democratic principles, the self-reliance of man, and his integrity, I sincerely regret painting this dark but not yet hopeless picture. However, it is based on extensive evidence. And it shows an American liberalism which is dying, contaminated with Freudian ethics and affected with deep-seated permissiveness, both morally and politically.

A biologist who believes in the immortality of the soul and in the Supreme Power which guides and leads the psychic evolution of the human race, such a biologist cannot be, should not be a pessimist. He would refuse to accept that the negative, destructive Freudian ethic which has contaminated our liberal intellectuals would bring about the destruction of our nation. For the biologist knows that there is an inbred force in the living world, in man as such, and in a nation, which regulates and controls extreme and often dangerous deviations, morbid as they might be: homeostasis. Sooner or later this biological force, present both in the individual and in the nation, would try forcefully to stabilize the affected organism or nation and bring it to the normal healthy state.

And there are all the indications that the psychopathic stage

through which our country has been going is now being reversed and that our nation will soon regain its sanity, in spite
of all the enthusiasm of some political leaders supporting the
mental aberrations of our youth and intellectuals. Many pessimistic Americans ask themselves: don't the New Left and left-
liberals reduce to zero every hope that the recovery of America
is possible? "The Polish philosopher Lesik Kolakowski is completely right in regarding the new left—all that 'Mao-Tse-tung-
ing' youth who believe in salvation by dictatorship and violence
—as a symptom of illness and not the cure—a symptom of that
sinister illness which fifty years ago first struck Russia."[5]

Yes there is hope of our country's returning to sanity. For
there is growing a religious rebirth both in the West and in the
East. We witness in this country masses of youth who are
searching in religious faith for the answer to their questions of
purposefulness of man's existence. Even in Soviet Russia this
religious rebirth is visible in the leading writers who are rejecting the atheistic attitude of the communists. The Russian writer
of the last century, Fyodor Dostoyevsky, declared that there
exists only one idea without which human life is impossible:
the idea of the immortality of the soul.

In this book we have tried to prove, on the basis of biological
sciences, the truth of this thesis and to demonstrate that the
misery of man and the death of all that is decent in society is
unavoidable if we reject God's guidance in our affairs and deny
the immortality of the soul.

[5]Quoted from the article of Michayl Michaylov, *N. Y. Times,* July 28, 1971.

Index

Index

Christian Jr./Sr High School
2100 Greenfield Dr
El Cajon, CA 92019

DATE DUE
